ヘルシング

HELLSING

4
FOUR

KOHTA HIRANO
平野耕太

translation
DUANE JOHNSON

lettering and retouch
WILBERT LACUNA
and STUDIO CUTIE

DARK HORSE MANGA

president and publisher
MIKE RICHARDSON

US editor
JUDY KHUU

first edition editors
TIM ERVIN *and* **FRED LUI**

associate editor
ROSE WEITZ

collection designer
SKYLER WEISSENFLUH

digital art technician
ADAM PRUETT

English-language version produced by DARK HORSE MANGA.

HELLSING vol. 4 by KOHTA HIRANO

Dark Horse Manga
A division of Dark Horse Comics LLC
10956 SE Main Street
Milwaukie OR 97222

DarkHorse.com

To find a comics shop in your area, visit comicshoplocator.com

Second edition: March 2024
Ebook ISBN 978-1-50673-862-8
Trade Paperback ISBN 978-1-50673-853-6

1 3 5 7 9 10 8 6 4 2
Printed in the United States of America

Library of Congress Cataloging-in-Publication Data

Names: Hirano, Kohta, author. | Johnson, Duane, 1976- translator. | Lacuna, Wilbert, illustrator. | Studio Cutie, illustrator.
Title: Hellsing / Kohta Hirano ; translation, Duane Johnson ; lettering and retouch, Wilbert Lacuna and Studio Cutie.
Other titles: Herushingu. English
Description: Second edition. | Milwaukie OR : Dark Horse Manga, 2023- | Summary: "The manga that spawned the worldwide hit anime, Kohta Hirano's Hellsing blends gothic horror, violent action, and dark humor into a bloody brew that has fired the imagination of otaku everywhere. This new edition features translation revisions to bring Hellsing even closer to Hirano's terrifying vision"-- Provided by publisher.
Identifiers: LCCN 2023014695 (print) | LCCN 2023014696 (ebook) | ISBN 9781506738505 (v. 1 ; trade paperback) | ISBN 9781506738598 (v. 1 ; ebook)
Subjects: LCGFT: Comics (Graphic works) | Vampire comics. | Horror comics. | Graphic novels. | Manga.
Classification: LCC PN6790.J33 H5648613 2023 (print) | LCC PN6790.J33 (ebook) | DDC 741.5/952--dc23/eng/20230605
LC record available at https://lccn.loc.gov/2023014695
LC ebook record available at https://lccn.loc.gov/2023014696

HELLSING

ヘルシング

IV

平野耕太

KOHTA HIRANO

CONTENTS

ORDER 19

WHAT'S THE MOST DREADFUL MONSTER THERE IS?
DO YOU KNOW, INTEGRA?
...THE VAMPIRE.
INDEED, THAT IT IS. OUR ARCH ENEMY IS THE VAMPIRE, INTEGRA.
SO, WHY IS THE VAMPIRE SO TERRIBLE?
THE VAMPIRE IS FULL OF WEAKNESSES. IT DETESTS GARLIC AND CROSSES. EUCHARIST WAFERS AND HOLY WATER BURN ITS FLESH.
IT CAN'T CROSS RIVERS, OCEANS, LAKES, OR FLOWING CANALS. IT CAN'T LOOK AT THE SUN OR LISTEN TO SCRIPTURE.
MOST VAMPIRES MOVE ONLY AT NIGHT. THEIR SOLE NEST OF REPOSE IS A SMALL, DARK COFFIN.

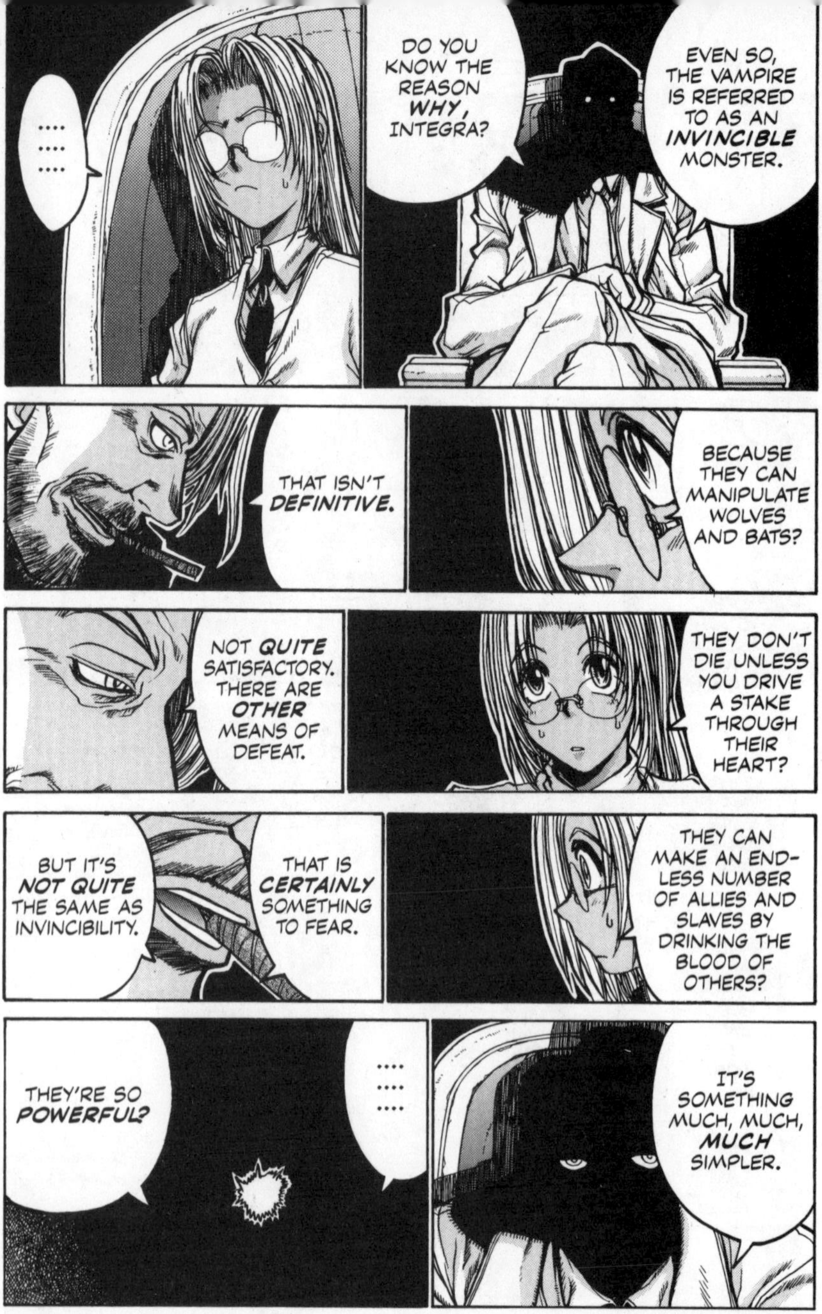
EVEN SO, THE VAMPIRE IS REFERRED TO AS AN INVINCIBLE MONSTER.
DO YOU KNOW THE REASON WHY, INTEGRA?
....
....
....
BECAUSE THEY CAN MANIPULATE WOLVES AND BATS?
THAT ISN'T DEFINITIVE.
THEY DON'T DIE UNLESS YOU DRIVE A STAKE THROUGH THEIR HEART?
NOT QUITE SATISFACTORY. THERE ARE OTHER MEANS OF DEFEAT.
THEY CAN MAKE AN END-LESS NUMBER OF ALLIES AND SLAVES BY DRINKING THE BLOOD OF OTHERS?
THAT IS CERTAINLY SOMETHING TO FEAR.
BUT IT'S NOT QUITE THE SAME AS INVINCIBILITY.
IT'S SOMETHING MUCH, MUCH, MUCH SIMPLER.
....
....
....
THEY'RE SO POWERFUL?

YES, THAT'S IT.
THE VAMPIRE IS EXCEEDINGLY POWERFUL, INTEGRA.
EXCELLENT REFLEXES AND CONCENTRATION, A SIXTH SENSE, PHYSICAL ADEPTNESS, SPECIAL ABILITIES, ENDURANCE, BLOOD SUCKING, TRANSFORMATION, AN UNDYING NATURE, ETC., ETC.
BUT WHAT IS MOST DREADFUL IS THAT BASIC VIOLENCE... POWER.
THEY TEAR THROUGH HUMANS LIKE THEY WERE MERE RAGS.
NOW, THE PROBLEM IS THAT THE VAMPIRE REALIZES IT POSSESSES THIS POWER.
NOT CONTENT WITH SIMPLICITY, BY THEIR LOGIC THEY WIELD POWER AS IF THEY WERE TYRANTS.
CLOSE-RANGE FIGHTING WITH VAMPIRES EQUALS DEATH.
UNDERSTAND, INTEGRA? VAMPIRES ARE INTELLIGENT, BLOOD-SUCKING FIENDS. THAT IS WHY THEY ARE THE MOST DREADFUL.

ORDER 19
エレベーター アクション
ELEVATOR ACTION⑥

SQUEAL LIKE A PIG? I WILL?
YOU STILL DON'T UNDERSTAND? SO DENSE, ALUCARD.
HAVE YOU GONE COMPLETELY SOFT IN THE HEAD?!
WHOO
SHM
SHM
SHM
SHM
キュゴゴゴゴゴ
EHH?!
ドドド
BROSH

KBOOM
FWAAAAA
ZMMMMMM
RUNNING AGAIN?! SO FUTILE...
POMM
!!

バキン!!
BKANG
ズワァァァァァァ
ZHWAAAAAAA
GSHAK
HELLSING FIRES MONDOLLAL

BOOM
BOOM
BOOM
BOOM
BOOM
BOOM
BOOM
BDOOM
BDOOM
BDOOM
BDOOM

GING GING GING GING GING
STUUUPIIIID LITTLLLLLE BIIIITCH!!
DON'T
FUCK
WITH
MEEEEEEE!
KRAK KRAK KRAK KRAK KRAK KRAK

GCHIK GCHIK
GCHIK GCHIK
FLING
VWMM
BWOOM

WHOO
DOOOON'T FUUUUCK
WIIIIITH MEEEEEE!!
SHRAK

ツパッ
SHAK
ドブァン
BDOOM
HNGUH?!
ブワァッ
VWAAAAA
HAHH!
IMPUDENT TRICKERY!!

ZMMMM
SHMM
!!
SHKK
?!
VWAAAAAA
GCHAK

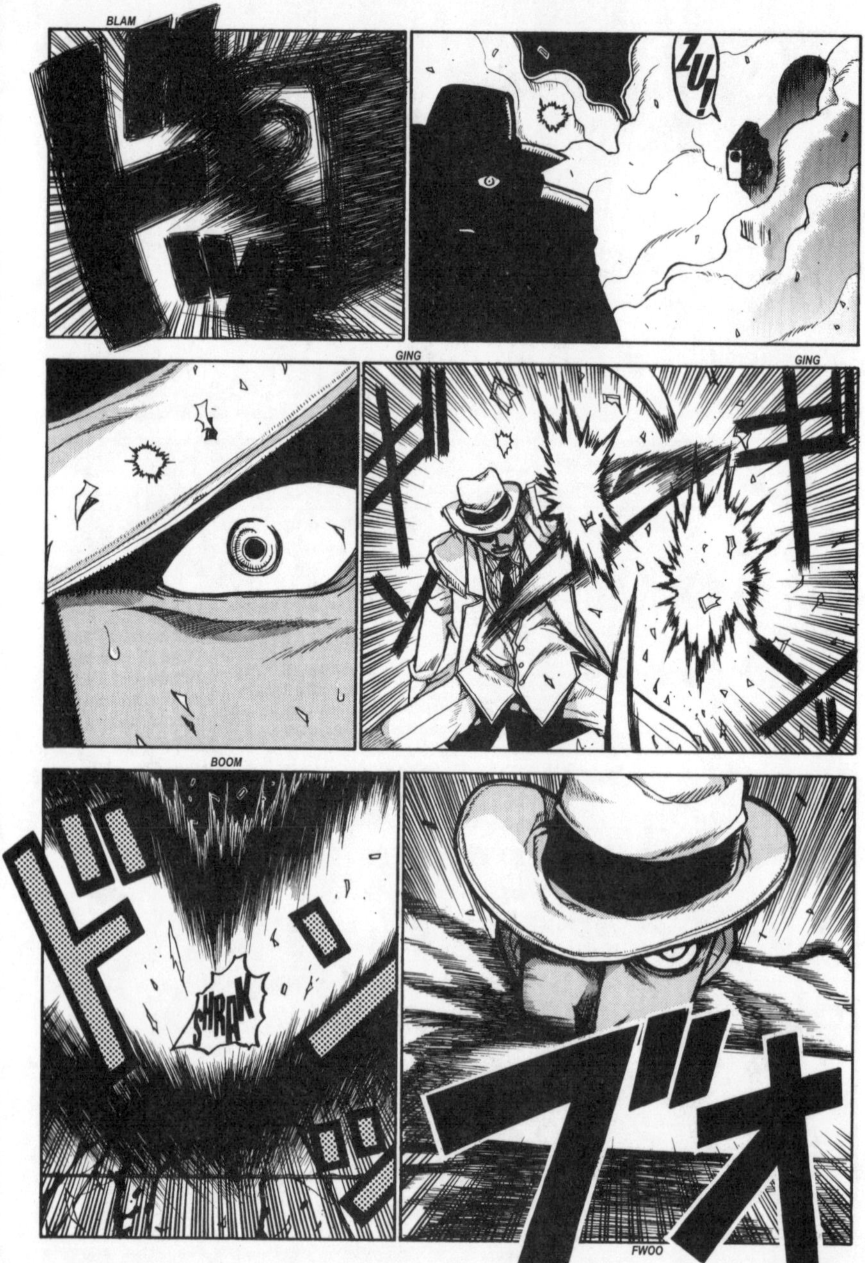

BLAM
ZU!
GING
GING
BOOM
SHRAK
FWOO

GACH GACH
ガチ
ガチ
GACH GACH
ガチ
ガチ
ガチ
ガチ
GACH GACH GACH GACH
ガチ
ガチ
ガチ
ガチ
シュオオオオオオオ
SHOOOOO
ユラッ
SWAY
HNAHH!
ヒュッッ
WHOOO

GRAB
KRAK
CRICK CRACK
POP
CRUNCH!
CRUNCH
SNAP
CRICK
SHRRRIP
GAH!
AH... GAHAH!
AH

NOW SQUEAL.
LIKE A PIG.

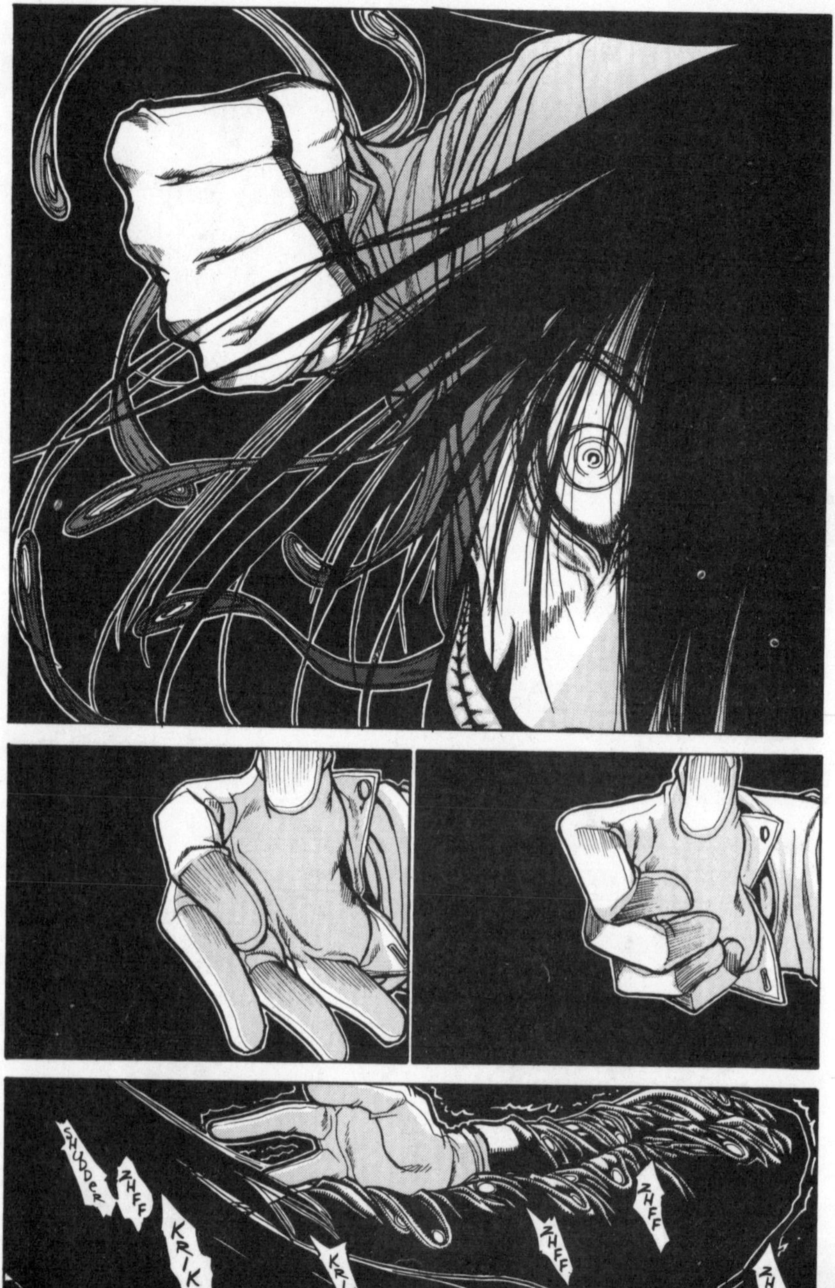
SHUDDER
ZHFF
KRIK
KRI
ZHFF
ZHFF
ZH

WHOOM
HN!
OH!
OHH!
VWOO

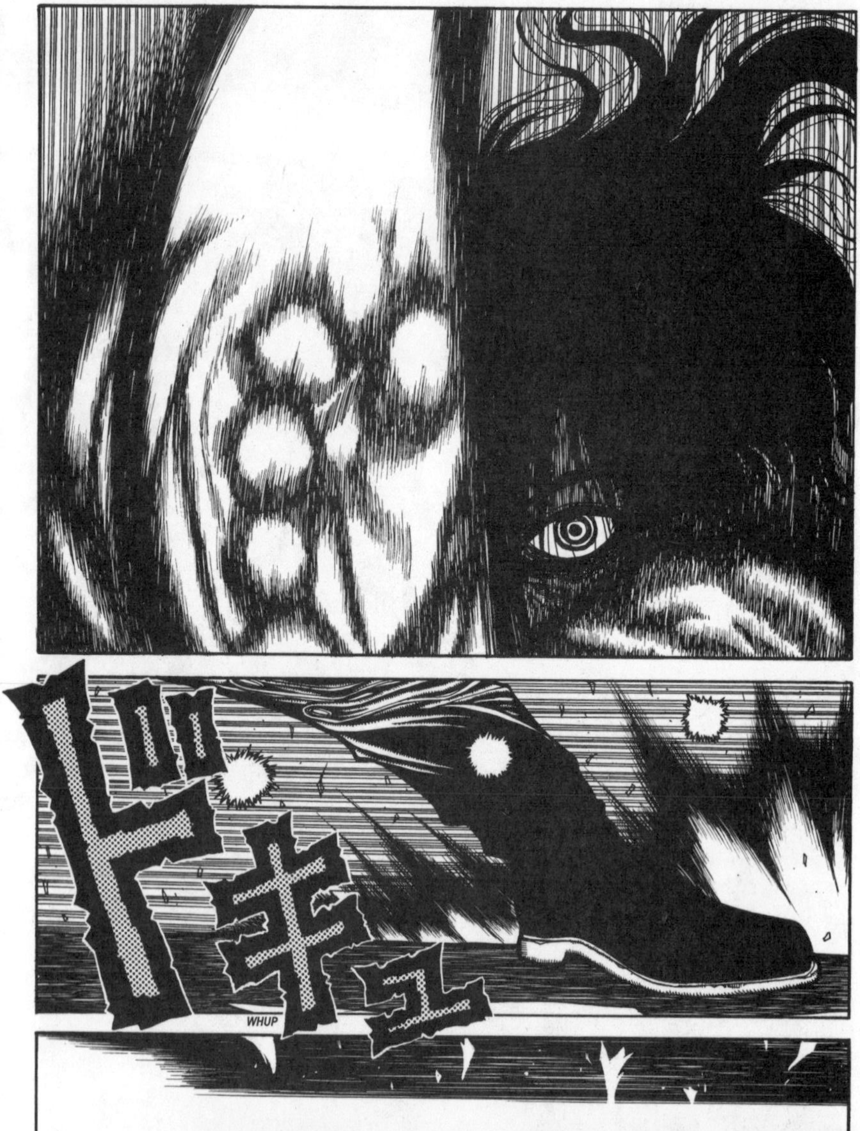
WHUP

POWW
SHRIP
RIP
CHRIP
SHREDD

GUCH
GUCH
GUCH

CHECKMATE, "DANDY."
NOW, FULFILL YOUR ARRANGEMENT WITH ME.
ALLOW ME TO COMPLETE MY MISSION.
I'LL HAVE YOU TELL ME EVERYTHING.
WITH YOUR LIFE...
SHOVE
OBF!

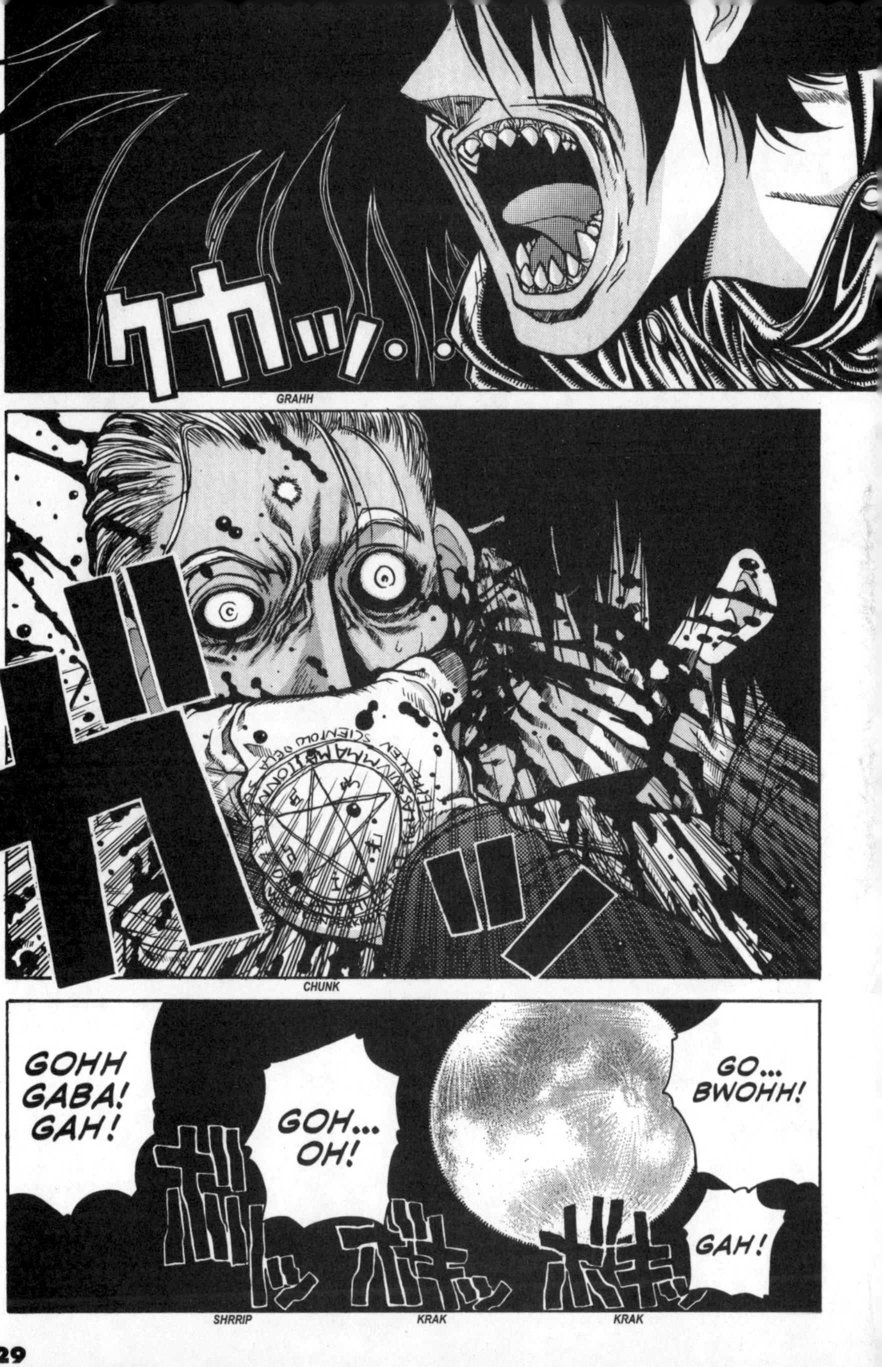
GRAHH
CHUNK
GO... BWOHH!
GAH!
GOH... OH!
GOHH GABA! GAH!
KRAK
KRAK
SHRRIP

OWAAH!
GOH!
SPLURT
Heil!!
Sie! Verzeihung Meine Kommandant!
WSSS
BROOSH

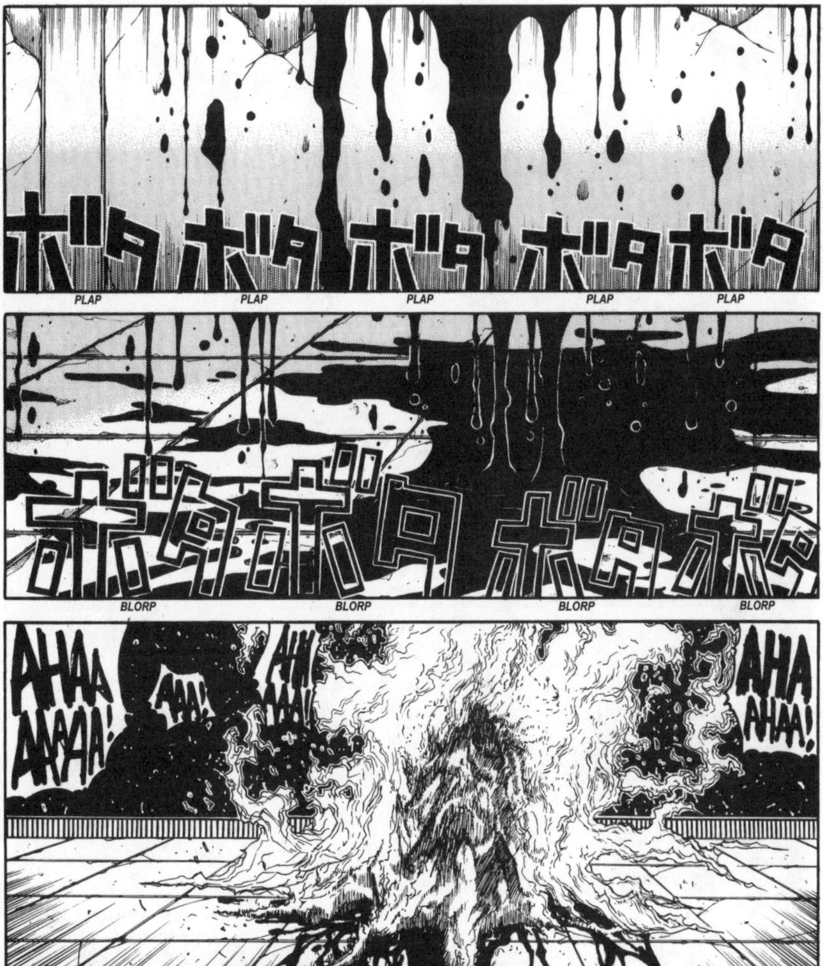

ボタボタ ボタ ボタボタ
PLAP
PLAP
PLAP
PLAP
PLAP
ボタボタ ボタボ
BLORP
BLORP
BLORP
BLORP
AHA AHAA!
AHH AAA!
AAA!
AHAA AAAHA!

BROOAR

HA!! HAAAAA!

M-
M--!
MASTERRR!
!!

PAP!
PAP!
PAP!
PAP!
PAP!
PAP!
PAP!
PAP!
PAP!
PAP!
GULP!

バタバタバタ
バタバタバタ
BADDA BADDA
BADDA BADDA
BADDA BADDA
バタバタバタバタ
TONK TONK
BADDA
BADDA
BADDA
BADDA
!!
コンコン
バタバタ
BADDA
BADDA

BADDA BADDA BADDA
バタ バタ バタ
ALUCARD, SIR!
SERAS, GIRL!
バタ バタ バタ
BADDA BADDA BADDA
GET CLOSE BY ZEM!!
ZERE!! PUT DOWN ZERE, NOW!!
Y-Y-YES SIR!
RIGHT AWAY!
OH, THE COMMANDER!
WHAT ABOUT THE COFFINS?
AH!... R-RIGHT!

ALUCARD, SIR! DO 'URRY UP, WE'RE SHORT ON TIME!
'URRY UP! COME ON, WHAT'RE YOU DOING?!
SIRRR!
KILLING OFF OUR ENEMIES, OUR ALLIES, THOSE WE SHOULD PROTECT, NATIONS WE SHOULD RULE, EVEN OURSELVES, BUT IT'S STILL NOT ENOUGH.
YOUR LOT AND I TRULY ARE INCORRIGIBLE WARMONGERS. AREN'T WE, MAJOR?
ORDER 19 / END

ORDER 20
エージ オブ エンパイア
AGE OF EMPIRE①

AND SO, THOSE OF YOU IN THE EUROPEAN OFFICE OF THE VATICAN AT THE TIME *AIDED* HIM AND HIS AGENCY.
OF COURSE, OF COURSE. YOU ARE NO DOUBT *CORRECT*, YOUR GRACE.
WITH A DECREE IN HAND FROM JUST BELOW HIS FÜHRER...
HE SOUGHT OUT OUR COOPERATION.
NO, HE *COERCED* US INTO COOPERATING!!

"ALWAYS WITH THAT LEERING GRIN AND THOSE UNPLEASANT EYES.
"THAT *DETESTABLE* GRIN THAT WOULD SEEM TO ALMOST SPLIT HIS CHEEKS.
"EVEN *NOW* WHEN I LOOK BACK ON IT, HE WAS A TRULY *DISGUSTING* MAN.
"*THIS* IS WHAT HE SAID... TO '*SAVOR THE JOY OF WAR LIMITLESSLY... FOR THE NEXT WAR, AND THE NEXT, AND THE NEXT.*'
"THIS SHORT, FAT, BESPECTACLED MERE LIEUTENANT SPOKE WITH THE AIR OF... ALMOST OF A COMMANDER OF HELL'S OWN MINIONS."

SO FROM THERE, THEY INITIATED THEIR OPERATION WITH *MUCH* GUSTO.
ON THE SURFACE... EVEN BENEATH THAT, IT WAS A PROJECT TO TRANSPORT MATERIALS AND PERSONNEL FROM THE OCCUPIED TERRITORIES. BUT THAT WAS NOT ALL...
COMPARED WITH *THIS*, SUCH A THING IS NOTHING MORE THAN TRIVIAL.
...!!
WHA-- ?!
TO BEGIN WITH, THOSE TRANSPORTED MATERIALS...
...WERE NOTHING MORE THAN CAPITAL FOR *THIS*.
CLICK CLICK CLICK CLICK
THE *"VAMPIRE PRODUCTION PROGRAM."*
CODE NAMED *LETZTES BATAILLON*.
(LAST BATALLION)
FLIT

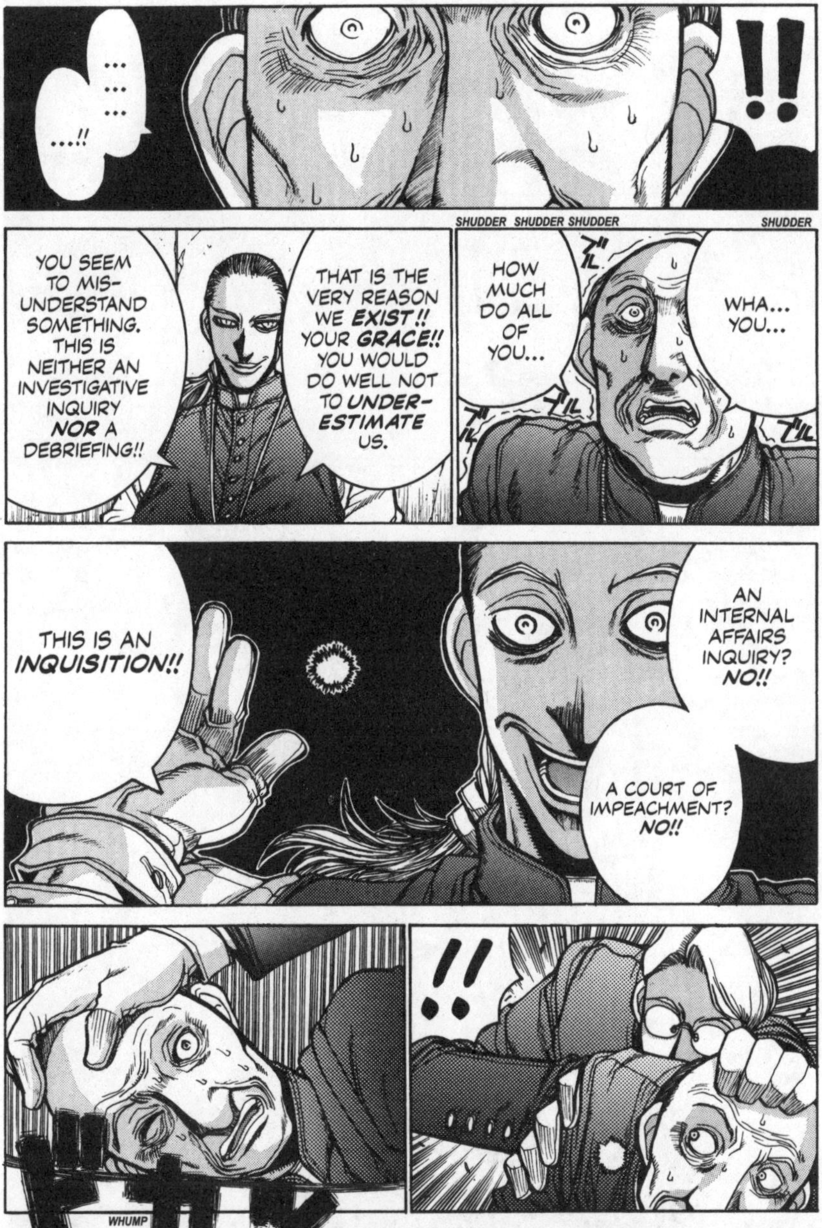

!!
...
...
...
...!!
SHUDDER SHUDDER SHUDDER
SHUDDER
WHA... YOU...
HOW MUCH DO ALL OF YOU...
THAT IS THE VERY REASON WE *EXIST!!* YOUR *GRACE!!* YOU WOULD DO WELL NOT TO *UNDER-ESTIMATE* US.
YOU SEEM TO MIS-UNDERSTAND SOMETHING. THIS IS NEITHER AN INVESTIGATIVE INQUIRY *NOR* A DEBRIEFING!!
AN INTERNAL AFFAIRS INQUIRY? *NO!!*
A COURT OF IMPEACHMENT? *NO!!*
THIS IS AN *INQUISITION!!*
!!
WHUMP

THEY COERCED YOU?! ABSURDITY!! ALL OF YOU GLADLY OFFERED YOUR ASSISTANCE!!
A PRO-NAZI SECT? PRO-GERMAN? NO!! WRONG!!
YOU WANTED TO BECOME VAMPIRES... DIDN'T YOU?!
HIS HONEYED WORDS AWOKE THE DESIRE WITHIN YOU AND YOU ACTED.
YOU WANTED IT BADLY ENOUGH TO TURN YOUR BACK ON GOD...
...AND SELL YOUR SOUL?! FOR A THING LIKE THAT?! A BISHOP SHOULD KNOW BETTER!!
HOWEVER, THE VAMPIRE RESEARCH WAS NOT COMPLETED IN TIME.
ALL THAT WAS ULTIMATELY PERFECTED WERE IMPERFECT GHOULS.
EVEN SO, THE ABILITY TO PLACE GHOULS AT THE FRONT LINES WOULD HAVE BEEN FEARFUL INDEED...
HAD THE PROGRAM NOT BEEN ESTROYED...

...BY HELLSING.
I-I-I...
I WAS... DE... DECEIVED!
IT WAS HIM! IT WAS HIS FAULT!
IT'S NOT JUST ME! NOT JUST...
THEY GOT TO... TO ALL OF US BACK THEN!!
IT PAINS ME TO THINK, EVEN FOR AN INSTANT, THAT A BISHOP DID THIS. YOUR GRACE...
YOU REALLY SHOULD TRY TO CONTAIN YOURSELF.
PLEASE, HAVE MERCY ON ME!
MAXWELL! FOR THE LOVE OF GOD!
I... I...!

UNFORTU-
NATELY...
I CANNOT.
GCHIK
IF YOU REALLY WERE A SERVANT OF GOD...
YOU'D KNOW THAT THE VATICAN COULD NEVER PERMIT YOUR SURVIVAL AFTER YOU SIDED WITH PEOPLE LIKE THEM.
AH!
AHA!
A! UAAA! AA!
AA!
AA!
Amen!

ORDER 20 / END

ORDER 21

WE HAVE RECEIVED FURTHER NEWS REGARDING THE HOTEL GUN BATTLE WHICH OCCURRED LATE LAST NIGHT.
BNB BRAZIL'S FERDOPACIEL COMES TO US LIVE FROM THE CHAOTIC SCENE IN FRONT OF THE HOTEL RIO.
GUN-GENOCIDE
LIO-SHOCK
BNB
SATELIGHT NEWS
BNB BLAZIL HEAD LINES
EVEN NOW THAT DAY HAS DAWNED, IT STILL LOOKS LIKE A BATTLEFIELD HERE IN FRONT OF THE HOTEL RIO...
...AS WELL AS WITHIN THE PERIMETER HOSPITAL CAMP.
GATE
107 ARE DEAD AND 64 WOUNDED IN THIS LARGE-SCALE INCIDENT.
THERE IS STILL NO KNOWLEDGE OF THE WHEREABOUTS OF THE PRINCIPAL OFFENDERS.

A HIJACKED CNNN NEWS HELICOPTER WAS UTILIZED IN THEIR ESCAPE.
IT WAS ABANDONED ON THE OUTSKIRTS OF THE CITY, BUT BY THE TIME OF ITS DISCOVERY IT WAS DESERTED.
THE PILOT WAS DISCOVERED STANDING IN A NEARBY FIELD, IN A STATE OF SHOCK.
MYSTERIOUSLY, THE PILOT HAS NO RECOLLECTION WHATSOEVER OF THE INCIDENT.
HE ISN'T EVEN ABLE TO COMPREHEND WHAT HE WAS DOING IN SUCH A PLACE.
GATE
AUTHORITIES ARE PROCEEDING WITH AN INVESTIGATION TO DETERMINE...
...WHETHER THE CRIMINALS USED SOME DRUG ON THE PILOT TO MANIPULATE HIS MEMORY.
DESPITE THE CONCERTED EFFORT OF EACH BRANCH OF THE POLICE FORCE, THE WHEREABOUTS OF THE CRIMINALS REMAINS A COMPLETE MYSTERY.
THIS IS FERDO PACIEL, REPORTING LIVE FOR BNB BRAZIL.
VSSH

ORDER 21
エージ オブ エンパイア
AGE OF EMPIRE②

AH HAH HAH HAH HAH HAH!
ALHAMBRA VAS NOTHING MORE THAN A DUST RAG.
I KNEW HE'D BE POWERFUL!!
RIDICULOUSLY POWERFUL!! MORE SO THAN VE IMAGINED!!
CLICK
M-M-MY... MY APOLOGIES. IT SEEMS... IT SEEMS I... I STILL DO NOT...
NEIN!!
DON'T BE FOOLISH. RATHER, THIS VAS CLOSE TO BEING A MAJOR SUCCESS.
HRRN HRRRRN
VITH THIS, VE HAVE MADE DEFINITE GAINS REGARDING THE ALUCARD.
HE IS THE INTERMEDIARY OF THE VONDERFUL EXISTENCE.
MONSTERS!! UNHUMANS!! NIGHTBREED!! SPECTERS!! HETERO-MORPHS!!
EACH ONE SOMETHING OTHER THAN HUMAN.
MIDIANS!!
NAMELY, THE DESIRE VE HAF LABORED TOWARDS FOR HALF A CENTURY.

BUILDING MIDIANS. UNIFORMING MIDIANS. TRAINING MIDIANS. ORGANIZING MIDIANS. EQUIPPING MIDIANS. UTILIZING MIDIANS. COMMANDING MIDIANS...
VE VILL FINALLY ***COMMAND*** EVEN MIDIANS THEMSELVES. VE, THE ***LETZTES BATAILLON***.
THE END OF THE CENTURY VILL SURELY ALSO MEAN THE END OF THE VORLD, **DOK**.
Welcome to this crazy time♫ *WILKOMMEN ZU DIESER VERRÜCKTEN ZEIT*. ♫
YOU ARE ***CERTAINLY*** A FORMIDABLE GENIUS, MY GRAND PROFESSOR.
YOU HAF MY...
...UTMOST GRATITUDE!!
ズパッ
ZPAP

NOW, GENTLEMEN. OUR MOST DELIGHTFUL SHOW IS, FOR THE MOMENT, AT UN END.
ズッ
ZMM
BACK TO OUR BELOVED HOME.
LET US BE ON OUR VAY NOW.
ズズ
ZMZMM
ズズズゥ
ZM ZM ZMMM
ズズズズズ
ZM ZM ZM ZM ZM

CAPTAIN, PREPARE TO COME ABOUT. UND HURRY.
THE OLD OPERA HOUSE MEN HAF VAITED LONG ENOUGH.
PROCEED VITH ALL DUE SPEED. I'M SURE THEIR FACES ARE RED VITH ANGER AND VORRY.
HAHAHAHA
INDEED!! IT'S NO DOUBT ONE SERIOUS AFFAIR.
VE SHALL HURRY, HERR MAJOR!!
READY FOR PORT TURN.
FLAPS STARTING.
CONFIRM ALL FLAPS STARTING.
ALTITUDE GOOD.
TWENTY DEGREES TO PORT!!
BVOOO
OOOOO

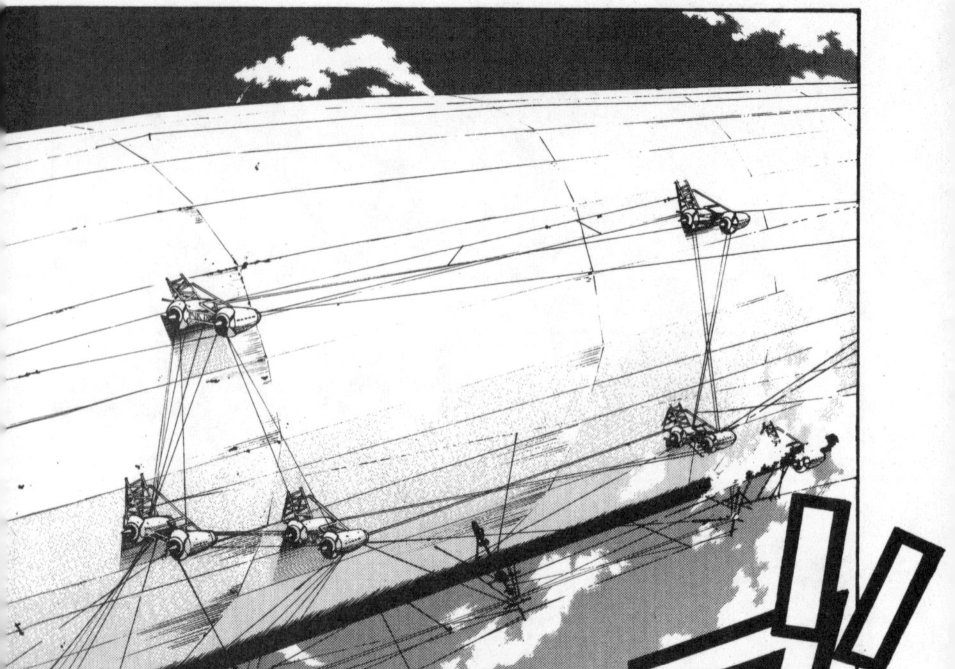
WHROOO

DESTINATION JABURO.
"THE PANTHER'S DEN."
LET'S DO THIS, OLD MEN. I DON'T CARE HOW MANY HUNDREDS, THOUSANDS, MILLIONS, OR BILLIONS HAF TO DIE IF THEY OPPOSE ME.
NEIN!!

GRAF ZEPPELIN
ALL WHO STAND IN THE VAY OF MY CONQUEST VILL DIE.

BRRRRRING
トゥルルルルル
KLIK
ガチャ
ALUCARD?!
WHEWW!
YES.
WHERE ARE YOU NOW?!
SOME REMOTE TOWN CALLED ST. ROSE OR SOMETHING, NEAR RIO.
Motel

I'VE COMPLETED MY MISSION, MY MASTER.
WHAT THEY'RE UP TO IS NOW ENGRAVED INTO MY BRAIN.
WELL DONE.
YESSS.
RETURN STRAIGHT AWAY. I EXPECT A FORMAL REPORT.
OHH?

IT SOUNDS LIKE THE ROUND TABLE COUNCIL'S TURNED UP THE HEAT.
IF ONLY THAT WAS THE WHOLE STORY.
IT'S A DIRECT ORDER FROM HIGHER UP.
HIGHER UP?
MEANING?
FROM HER MAJESTY HERSELF.
SHE'S CALLED THE COUNCIL TOGETHER.
HOHO!! THE QUEEN!!
YOU THINK THIS IS A LAUGHING MATTER?! YOU'RE MISTAKEN.
ESCAPE AND RETURN HOME IMMEDIATELY!! DO NOT MAKE HER WAIT.
YAHHH.
SECTION XIII IS MOVING AS WELL.
I HAVE NO DESIRE TO BE OUTDONE BY THEM!!

BY THE WAY, INTEGRA. HOW DID YOU LIKE THE JOY OF WAR? MISS DIRECTOR...
DID IT SET YOU ABOIL?
WERE YOU ABLE TO SEE THE DARK RED FLAMES BLAZING?
OH SHUT IT!! BLOODY FOOL, HOW WOULD I KNOW THAT?!
GET BACK HERE THIS INSTANT, YOU GIT!!
GCHAK!
HMHM HMHM HM.
AHAHAH AHAHAH.
SURELY, HUMANS ARE SO WONDERFULLY COMPLEX.
HMHA HAH!

GCHAK
HALLO, WE'RE BAAAAACK.
BON JOUUUUUR!
BTAMM
SURE ENOUGH, DIDN'T WORK. NOT A BIT. BAD IDEA FROM ANY ANGLE.
SLURRRP
THERE AREN'T ANY SHIPS LEAVING FOR A WEEK.
AND ANYWAY... THE SCHEDULE'S ALREADY BOOKED UP.
OUT OF THE QUESTION.
YOU TWO, GET READY.
EH?
WE'RE STEALING AN AIRPLANE.

THERE'S NO OTHER WAY.
GET READY.
FLY IN THE SKY
NON NON NON NON NON NON NON NON NON!
DEAD DEAD DEAD DEAD DEAD, ZIS TIME WE'RE DEAD!
AHHH, PULL ZE OZER ONE!
I'M GONNA DIE, I'M GONNA DIE, NO ZANKS, NOT FOR ME!
!!

?
スッ
SHPP
Sun-Lo
MOTEL
カッ
KATZ
カッ
KATZ
カッ
KATZ
カッ
KATZ
カッ
KATZ
カッ
KATZ
カッ
KATZ

!!!
?
HNGAH AHH!
!!!?!
ダッ
DASH
?!
BAMM
カッカッ カッカッ
KATZ KATZ KATZ KATZ
カッカッカッ カッカッ
KATZ KATZ KATZ KATZ KATZ

KATZ
KATZ
KATZ
KATZ
カッ
カッ
カッ
カッ
KATZ
KATZ
KATZ
KATZ
KATZ
カッ
カッ
カッ
カッ
カッ

Speak with the dead
AAAAAAAA
RAAAAAAAA
AAA

WHOKK

TREMBLE
TREMBLE
TREMBLE
TREMBLE
ビッ
ビッ
ビッ
ビッ
GEH AH!
-AHA!- -AH!-
-GNAH!-
ALUCARRRD!!
-GAH HAHH!-
COULDN'T STAND IT ANYMORE, AH?! ANDERSON!!
-HAH!-

WHPP
ZSHH
WHOM

BOKK

DOWWW

TREMBLE TREMBLE
TREMBLE
TREMBLE
TREMBLE
TREMBLE
GAH!
BAHA!
GEHAH!
GABO! HAH!
GAHAA HAHA HAH!
DAMN HUMAN!
HA HA HA HA!

CHAK KINNNG
ZPPP
ACH!
Shit Fuck!
KCHIKK

HNNNRAHHHHH!
!!
?!
!!
DEATH cannon
SUPER
TREMBLE
プル
TREMBLE
プル
TREMBLE
プル
TREMBLE
プル
TREMBLE
プル
TREMBLE
プル
AH.
プル
プル
プル

SHFF
すうっ
HMPH!
VNN
WHA!
AH!
WAH!
SHNKK

REACH
?!
!
ZMP
ZZZPPP
SHOOO

!
AIF YE GO ABOOT THIRTEEN KILOMETERS TIL THE NOORTH, THERE'S AE VATICAN AIRFIELD DISGUISED AS AE CROPDUSTER'S.
THERE'S AE WEE JET THERE WI' ITS ENGINE A'READY WARMED UP.
バタバタバ
バタ
FLAP
FLAP
FLAP
GING ON, AWAY WI YE.
IT'S A' YERS, TAK IT AND VANISH.
...WHILE AH CAN STILL CONTROL MA URGE TAE KILL THE LOT O' YE.
ORDER 21 / END

ORDER 22

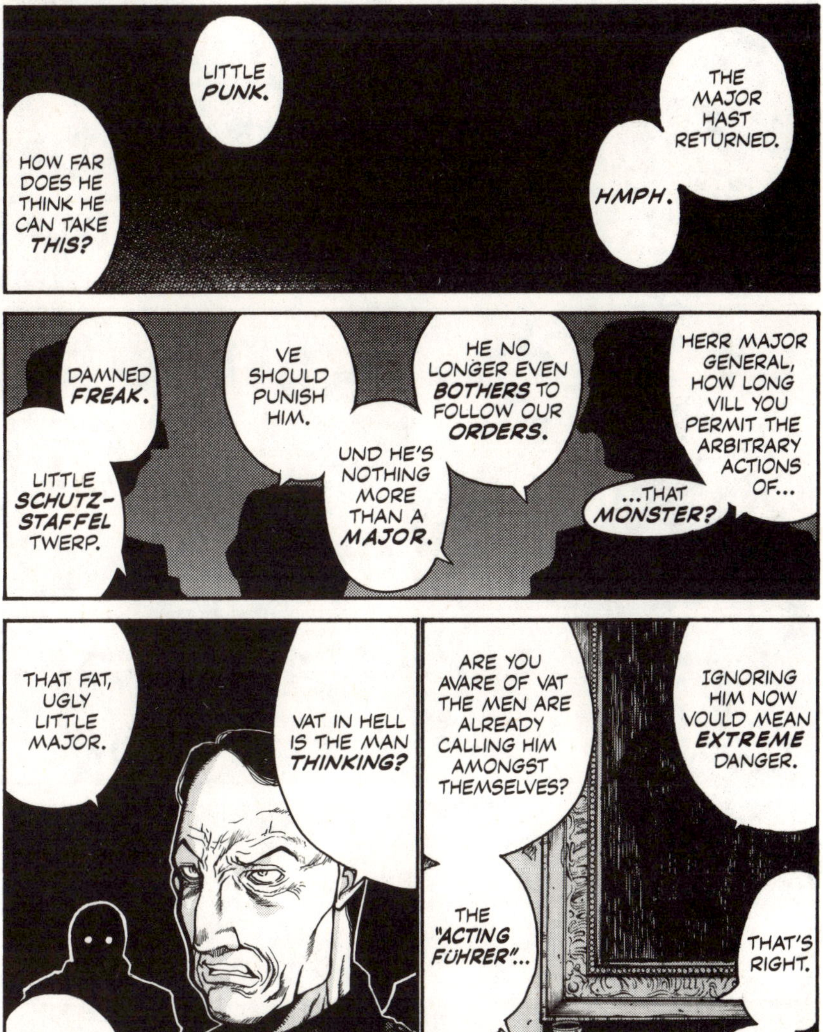
THE MAJOR HAST RETURNED.
HMPH.
LITTLE PUNK.
HOW FAR DOES HE THINK HE CAN TAKE THIS?
HERR MAJOR GENERAL, HOW LONG VILL YOU PERMIT THE ARBITRARY ACTIONS OF...
...THAT MONSTER?
HE NO LONGER EVEN BOTHERS TO FOLLOW OUR ORDERS.
UND HE'S NOTHING MORE THAN A MAJOR.
VE SHOULD PUNISH HIM.
DAMNED FREAK.
LITTLE SCHUTZ-STAFFEL TWERP.
IGNORING HIM NOW VOULD MEAN EXTREME DANGER.
ARE YOU AVARE OF VAT THE MEN ARE ALREADY CALLING HIM AMONGST THEMSELVES?
THE "ACTING FÜHRER"...
THAT'S RIGHT.
DEVILISH BASTARD.
A TASTE-LESS JEST...
VAT IN HELL IS THE MAN THINKING?
THAT FAT, UGLY LITTLE MAJOR.
FREAKS, EVERY SINGLE ONE OF THEM.

SCHNELL!
MACHT SCHNELL!
SCHNELL!
TMP
TMP
TMP
TMP
TMP
BACK EVEN...
...SOONER THAN I EXPECTED.
HERR MAJOR HAST RETURNED!
TRMP
TRMP
TRMP
TRMP
TRMP
FALL IN!!
FALL IN!!

ゴウゥン
GRRRRRN
ガタガタガタ
GTAK
GTAK
GTAK
ズウウウゥ
ZMMMMM
ズウウウウウ
ZMMMMMMM
ACHTUNG!!
HEIL THE COMMANDER OF THE LETZTES BATAILLON!
HEIL!!

ORDER 22
エージ オブ エンパイア
AGE OF EMPIRE③

VELCOME BACK, MAJOR.
HOW VAS YOUR VALK IN THE CLOUDS?
I GUESS IT MUST BE TOO STUFFY IN THIS CAVE, JA?
VITHOUT A DOUBT.
TUBALCAIN VAS BEATEN UND EATEN.
HOO?
I KNEW IT.

HIS OPPONENT VAS THE RENOWNED NOSFERATU ALUCARD. UND HE VAS JUST A CARD SHARK, EVEN IF HE VAS A VAMPIRE...
IT'S LIKE I TOLD YOU, JUST LEAVE IT TO US VEREVOLVES.
VE'LL MAKE SURE HE'S GOOOOD UND DEAD.
VARRANT OFFICER SCHRÖ-DINGER.
YOU KNOW NOT VAT YOU SAY.
COME, NO MATTER.
HOWEVER, THERE VERE RESULTS.

HEY, CAPTAIN.
YOU AGREE, RIGHT?
IF IT VERE US...
HELLSING VOULD NEVER...
SHIVER
AH... NEIN... UM.
I... I APOLOGIZE.
HERR MAJOR.
COME COME, DON'T ABASE YOURSELF SO.
IT'S DISGUSTING, CHIEF.
VAT ABOUT THE OTHER VEREVOLVES?

JAWOHL. VE DIDN'T THINK YOU VOULD ARRIVE BACK THIS SOON...
THEY'RE PROBABLY SCRAMBLING TO GET HERE.
I SEE, I SEE.
THE TIME HAST FINALLY COME, CHIEF.
♪
KREE KREE KREE KREE KREE KREE
キィッキィッキィッキィッキィッキィッ
MAJOR?!
THE TIME FOR VAT?

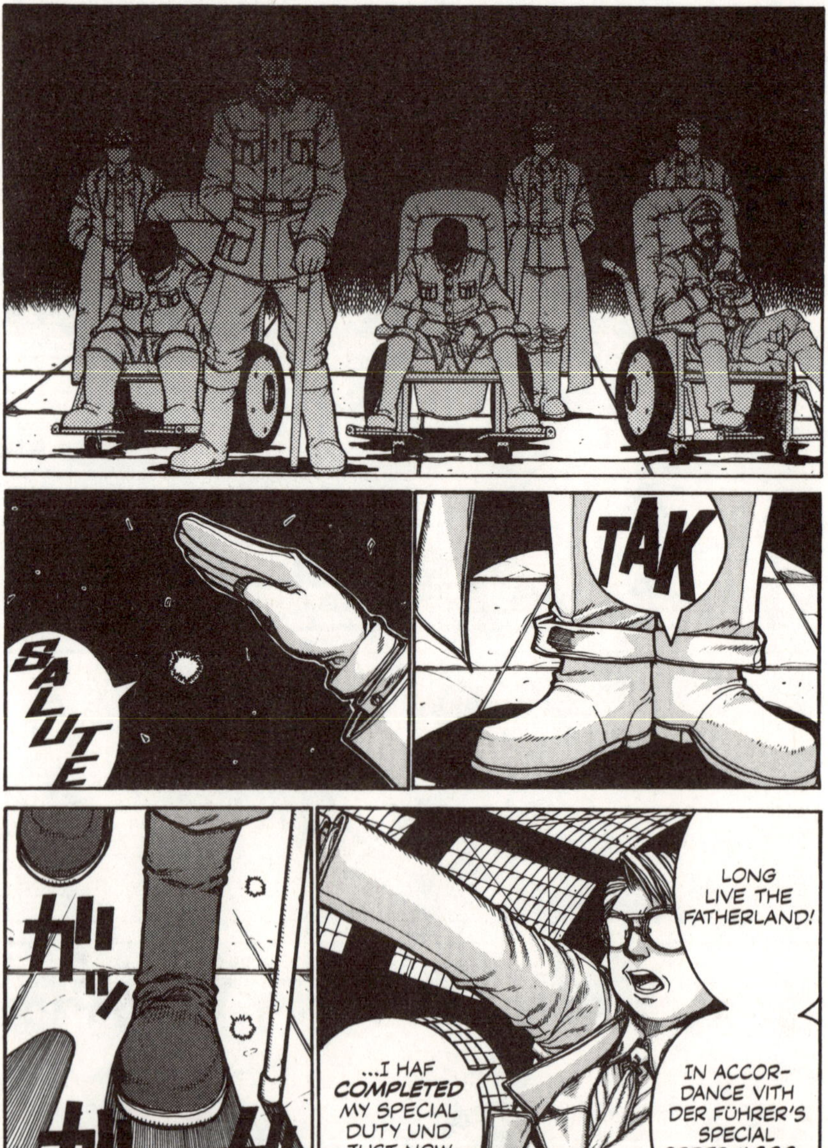

GATZ GATZ GATZ

VAT THE HELL ARE YOU DOING?!
YOU... ALL OF YOU...
I REALLY CANNOT ANSWER THAT QUESTION, HERR COLONEL.
UNDER SPECIAL ORDER FROM OUR LATE FÜHRER, I CANNOT DIVULGE SUCH INFORMATION NO MATTER HOW HIGHLY RANKED UN OFFICER ASKS ME.
THESE VEIGHTY INDISCRETIONS ARE IN DIRECT VIOLATION OF OUR ORDERS.
DER FÜHRER'S SPECIAL ORDER TAKES PRECEDENCE OVER ALL OTHER COMMAND STRUCTURES.
HOW DARE YOU TAKE THE TITLE OF FÜHRER UPON YOURSELF...
I AM NO MORE THAN A PETTY OFFICIAL FOLLOWING HIS ORDERS.

VELL, DON'T PRESUME THAT EVERYTHING VILL GO ACCORDING TO YOUR PLANS.
MAJOR.
IN THAT CASE, VHY DON'T YOU KISS MY OFFICIAL ASS?
HERR COLONEL.
HAHAHAHAHAHA
SWAKK
バギ

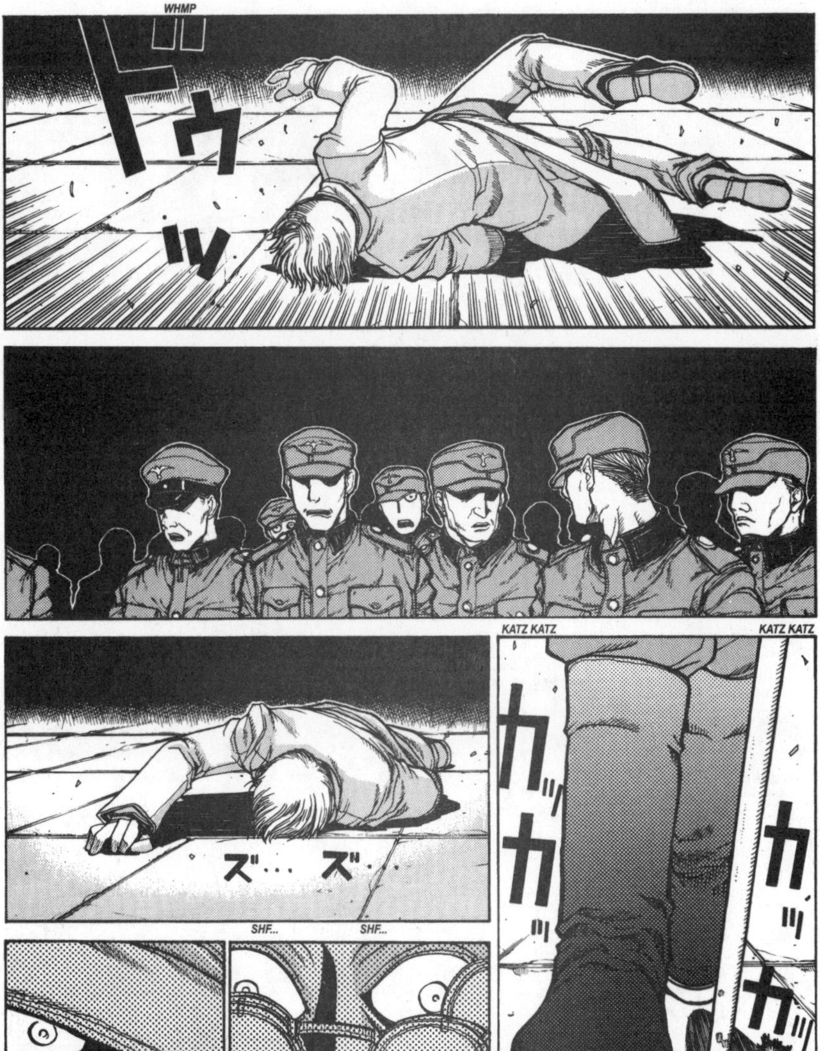
WHMP
ドゥッ
KATZ KATZ
カッカッ
KATZ KATZ
カッカッ
ズ…ズ…
SHF… SHF…

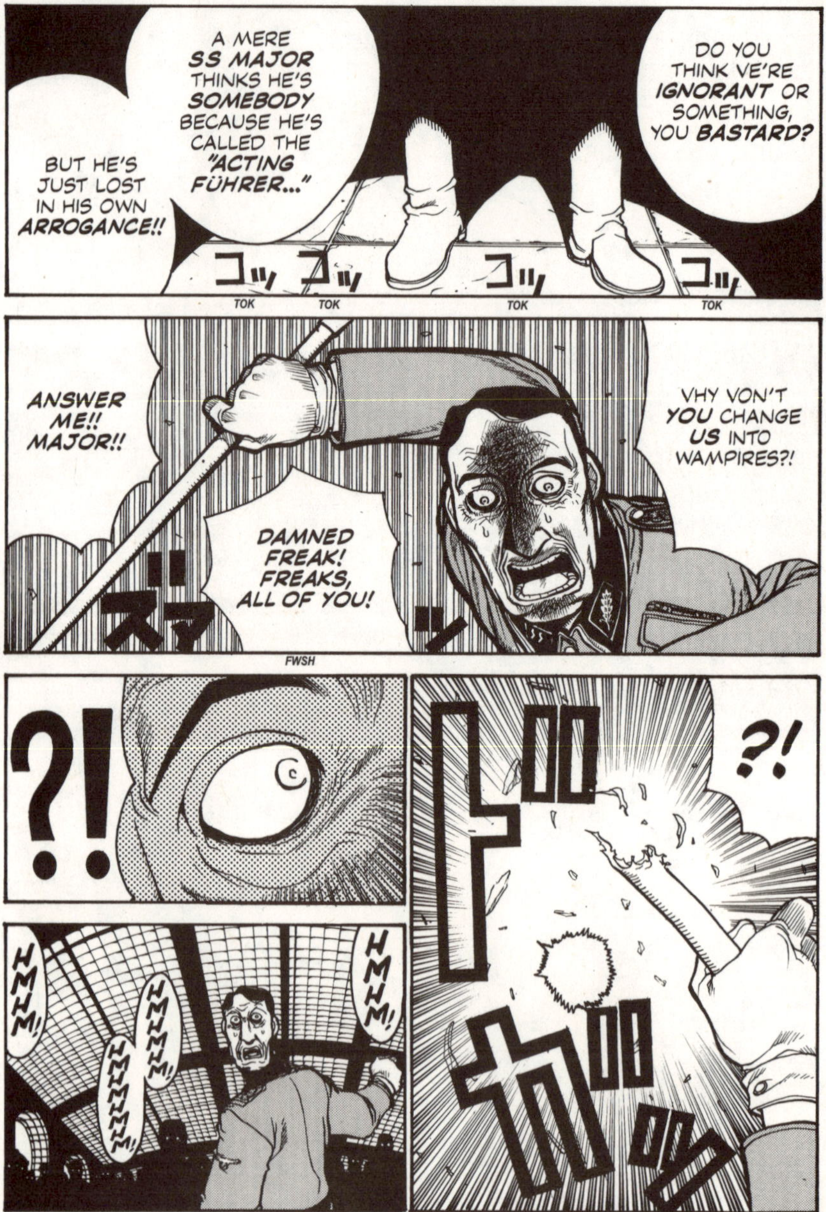
DO YOU THINK VE'RE IGNORANT OR SOMETHING, YOU BASTARD?
A MERE SS MAJOR THINKS HE'S SOMEBODY BECAUSE HE'S CALLED THE "ACTING FÜHRER..."
BUT HE'S JUST LOST IN HIS OWN ARROGANCE!!
TOK
TOK
TOK
TOK
VHY VON'T YOU CHANGE US INTO WAMPIRES?!
DAMNED FREAK! FREAKS, ALL OF YOU!
ANSWER ME!! MAJOR!!
FWSH
?!
BWHAM
?!
HMHM!
HMHMHM!
HMHMHMHM!
HMHM!

YOU VOULD DO VELL TO BACK DOWN, COLONEL.
THE MAJOR PREPARED AND BUILT UP BOTH MILLENIUM UND THE BATTALION IN THE FIRST PLACE.
YOU ALL ARRIVED AFTER THE FACT AND JUST HAPPENED TO HAF MORE STARS ON YOUR UNIFORMS.
IF THE FREELOADERS PUSH THEIR LUCK TOO FAR...
VE'LL KILL THEM ALL OFF... GRAMPS.
チリッ
CHING
チリッ
CHING
チリッ
CHING
チリッ
CHING
!!
!!
CHAK

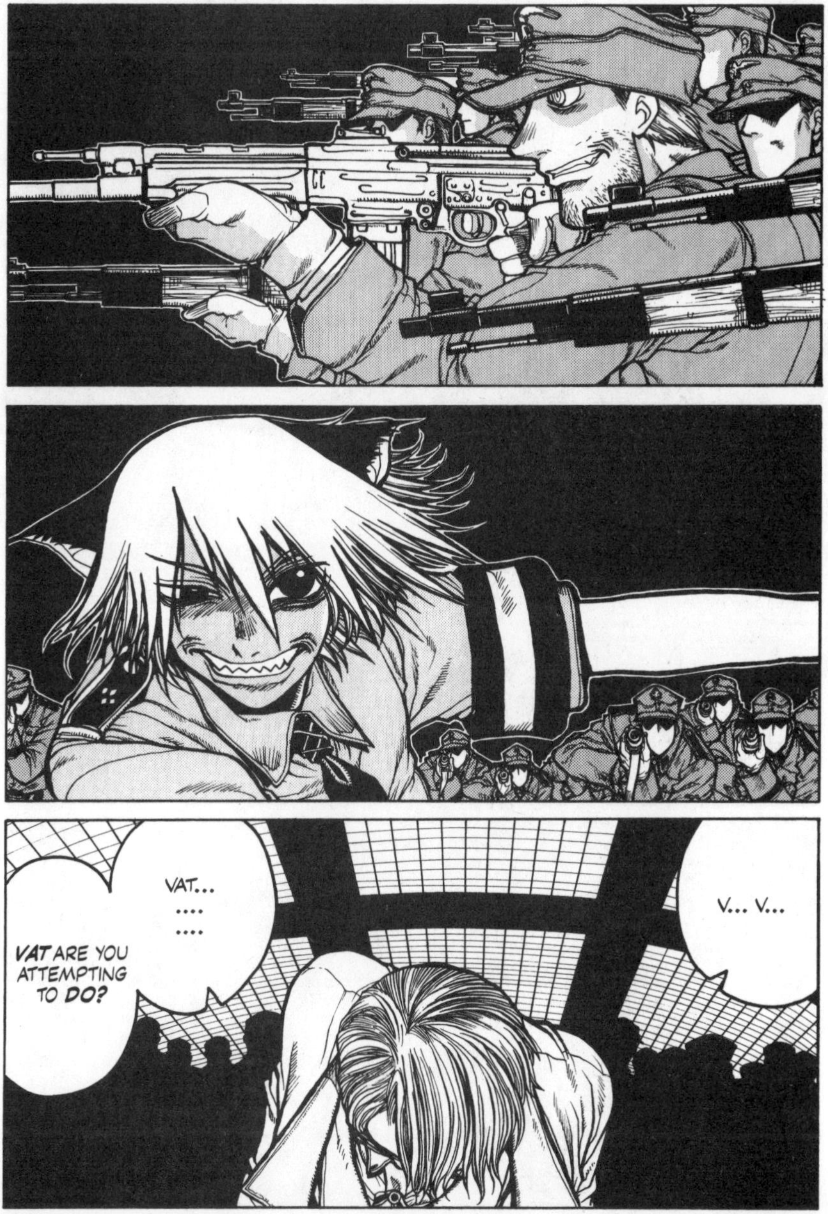
V... V...
VAT...
....
....
VAT ARE YOU ATTEMPTING TO DO?

VITH THIS BATTALION OF ONE THOUSAND WAMPIRES...

...VAT THE HELL DO YOU PLAN TO DO, MAJOR!?

MY OBJECTIVE?
ポタ
ポタ
ポタ
ポタタッ
HMHM, MY OBJECTIVE, HERR COLONEL?
PLIP
PLIP
PLIP
PLIPLAP
TO SAVOR THE JOY OF VAR LIMITLESSLY.
FOR THE NEXT VAR, UND THE NEXT, UND THE NEXT.
ORDER 22 / END

ORDER 23

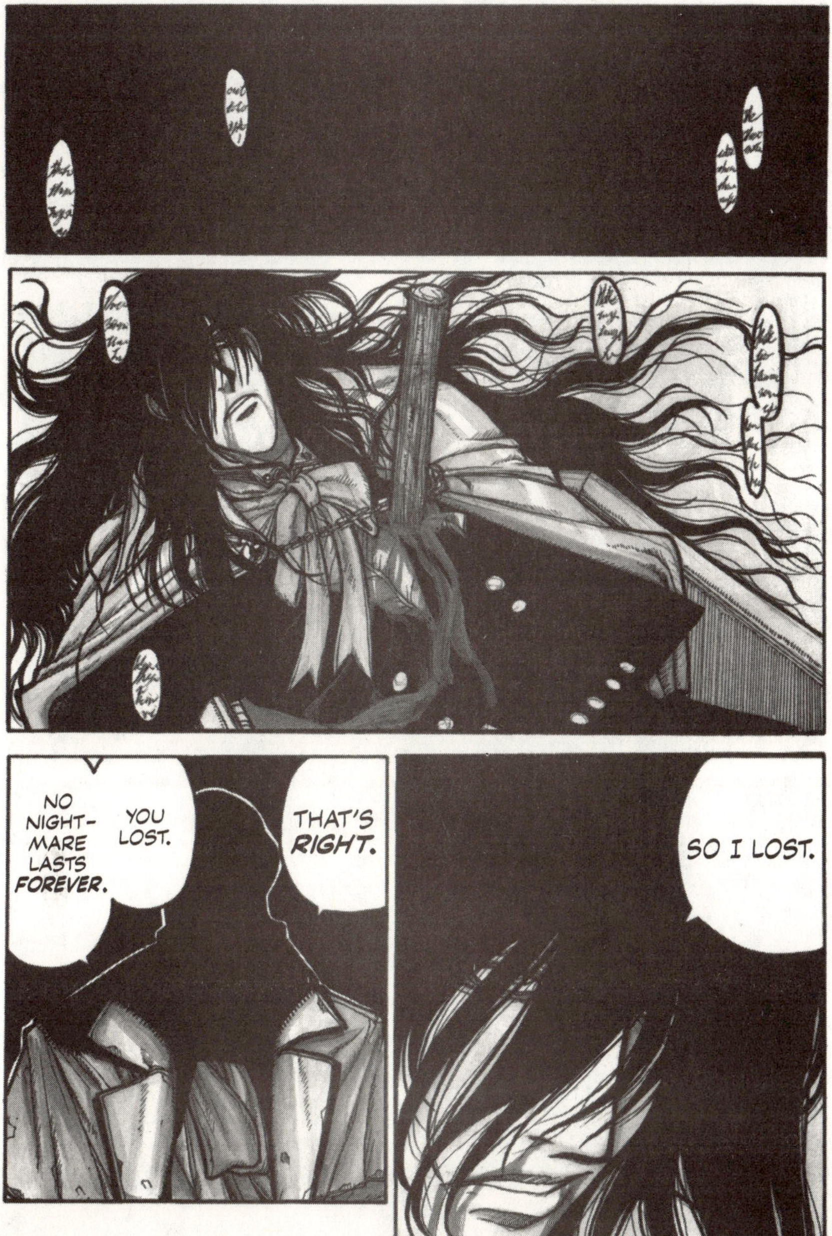

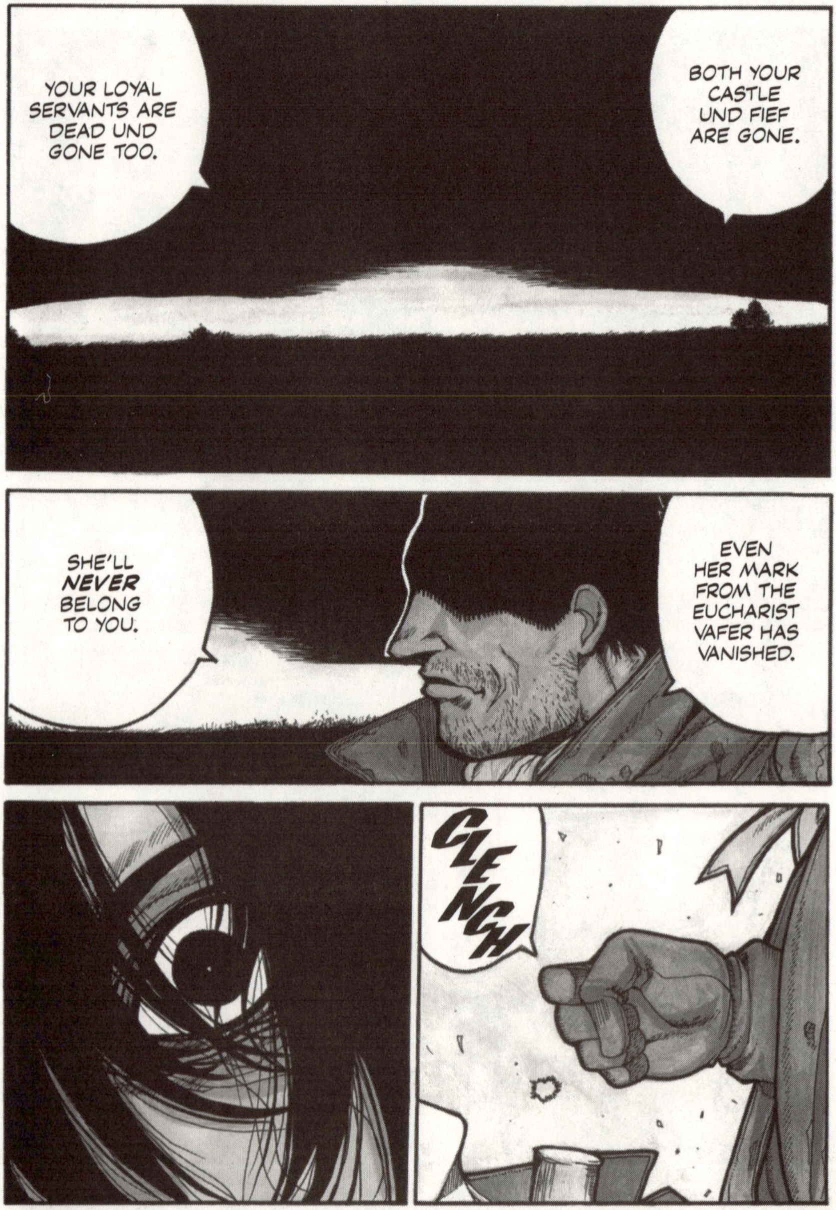
BOTH YOUR CASTLE UND FIEF ARE GONE.
YOUR LOYAL SERVANTS ARE DEAD UND GONE TOO.
EVEN HER MARK FROM THE EUCHARIST VAFER HAS VANISHED.
SHE'LL **NEVER** BELONG TO YOU.
CLENCH

MISERABLE NO LIFE KING! EVERYTHING YOU HAD IST NOW GONE!
YOU'VE GOT NOTHING LEFT NOW, COUNT!

ORDER 23
コールトゥパワー
CALL TO POWER

'ELLO, SIR! WE'LL BE IN ENGLAND AGAIN SOON ENOUGH.
LANDING IS IN TEN MINUTES, SO GET READY.
GOHHHHHHHHH
ZZZZZZZ
A DREAM.
ME?! DREAMING...?! HOW RIDICULOUS.
TOUCH

OUTSKIRTS OF LONDON, THE ROYAL FAMILY VILLA KRAUNEY HOUSE.

SIR HELLSING.
HAS HE STILL NOT ARRIVED YET?
YES, YOUR MAJESTY.
I BELIEVE HE WILL BE HERE VERY SOON NOW.

PERHAPS IT VAS A BAD IDEA TO USE ANDERSON AS MESSENGER?
NO.
UNFORTUNATELY, AND UNPLEASANTLY, WE ARE RUNNING IN CIRCLES WITH OUR HANDS TIED.
ALL OF OUR ACTIONS ARE COMPLETELY DEVOTED TO THESE PEOPLE.
WITHOUT A VERITABLE SURGE OF DILIGENCE, WE WILL NOT BE ABLE TO EVEN TOUCH THEM.
THEIR COLLABORATORS HAVE SPREAD EVERYWHERE.
GOVERNMENTS, MILITARIES, THE ECONOMIC WORLD, RELIGIONS, ETCETERA, ETCETERA.
THERE ARE FEW PEOPLE WHO CAN PREVAIL AGAINST THE TEMPTATION OF ETERNAL LIFE.
I SHOULD NOT BE SURPRISED IF THAT HOLDS TRUE WORLDWIDE, INCLUDING ENGLAND AND THE VATICAN.
AND PROBABLY EVEN AMONG THOSE HERE.
DAMNED VERMIN.

GCHAK
CRIKEY...
TRULY SPLENDID, EVERYONE'S HERE.
SMM
カッ
KATZ
カッカッ
KATZ KATZ

I HAVE JUST RETURNED...
MY MASTER.
YOU'VE DONE YOUR DUTY WELL...
MY SERVANT.
YOU STAND BEFORE THE QUEEN. REMOVE YOUR SUNGLASSES.
ZPP
KATZ KATZ KATZ
AH!
HEY!
GET BACK, YOU!
KATZ
KATZ
KATZ
KATZ

KAZ
スゥゥゥゥ
SHOOOO
......IT'S BEEN A LONG TIME...
...VAMPIRE.
YES, I SUPPOSE ABOUT FIFTY YEARS.
YOU'VE BECOME THE QUEEN SINCE THEN.
LET'S HAVE A LOOK AT YOUR FACE.
TOUCH

LOOK AT ME NOW. I'M ALREADY SO, SO OLD.
JUST A WRINKLED OLD WOMAN.
NOTHING ABOUT YOU EVER CHANGES, ALUCARD.
NO, NOW YOU ARE TRULY BEAUTIFUL, QUEEN.
YOU'RE STILL THAT SAME SAUCY FILLY FROM FIFTY YEARS AGO, YOUNG LADY.
VAMPIRE.
DELIVER YOUR REPORT...
HMHM.

ONCE UPON A TIME THERE WAS AN INSANE MAJOR IN THE SS.
HE SAID, "LET US MAKE AN IMMORTAL ARMY. LET US MAKE INVULNERABLE SOLDIERS."
THEY STROVE TOWARDS THEIR RECKLESS GOAL IN A SWELLING SEA OF BLOOD AND MADNESS.
AND THAT WOULD BE THE MILLENIUM ORGANIZATION'S PROJECT.
CORRECT. BUT FIFTY-FIVE YEARS AGO...
WE PUT AN END TO THAT PROJECT.
"WE" BEING MYSELF AND WALTER.
HOWEVER...

EVERYONE FORGOT ABOUT THEM, OR *TRIED* TO.
BUT THEY UNDOUBTEDLY CONTINUE THEIR *VINDICTIVE EXISTENCE* IN THE DEPTHS OF SHADOW.
WHILE SLOWLY, SLOWLY *EXTENDING* THEIR ABILITIES.
THEY DIDN'T ABANDON THEIR *TRUE* INTENTION.
SURELY *THIS* IS THE RETURN OF *SIEGFRIED'S MYTHICAL FORCE.*
A VAMPIRE KAMPF GRUPPE, AN INVULNERABLE ARMY OF UNHUMANS.
CURRENTLY, THEIR *DREADFUL* RESEARCH IS REACHING ITS HORIZON OF PERFECTING VAMPIRE PRODUCTION.
THE LAST TROOP REMNANTS OF *THE THIRD REICH.*
THE LETZTES BATAILLON.

MURMUR
MURMUR
MURMUR
MURMUR
ざわ ざわ ざわ ざわ
GRIN
TUBALCAIN'S BLOOD SHOWED ME THE VAY HERE.
!!
?!
REALLY... I GUESS HE VAS GOOD FOR SOME-THING...!!

WHIP
ヒュパッ!!
WHIP
ズパッ!!
FWIT
ピタ
VAIT.
I'M JUST A MESSENGER.
I'M NOT HERE TO FIGHT YOU.
MESSENGER?
WHEN DID YOU...? WHERE DID YOU...?
WALTER?!
OUR SECURITY WAS FLAWLESS.
NOR ARE THERE ANY SIGNS OF BREAK-IN.
SAVE YOUR BREATH.

I'M EVERYVHERE.
AND NOVHERE.
SHF
EVEN A LAD LIKE THAT?!
MILLENIUM... THE LETZTES BATAILLON... WHAT ON EARTH DO THEY AIM TO DO?
SINCE EVERYVONE FROM ENGLAND UND THE VATICAN ARE GATHERED TOGETHER HERE TODAY...
...OUR KOMMANDANT, HERR MAJOR, HAS SOMETHING VERY IMPORTANT TO SAY. SO PLEASE, SIT BACK UND LISTEN.
TNK

BAM
HAH!
...
WHAT?
GUTEN TAG.
[surprise]
HNNNN
RIGHT, GOOD DAY.
BOW

CLICK
CLICK CLICK
EH?
VARRANT OFFICER SCHRÖDINGER, THIS ISN'T VORKING AT ALL.
AHH? VAT'S WRONG, THERE'S NO SIGNAL.
MAJOR! STOP THIS! STOP, FOR GOD'S SAKE...!
VAT ARE YOU DOING? HURRY UND STAND HERR BRIGADIER GENERAL UP AGAINST THE VALL.
MAJOR! PLEASE, SAVE US! SA...
HM, AHH. THERE'S THE IMAGE.
BANG BANG BANG

!!
?!
!!
BUT NOW I FINALLY FIND RELIEF.
SOUNDS LIKE YOU HAF YOUR HANDS FULL THERE, MAJOR.
IT'S TROUBLE-SOME HAVING TO DEAL VITH SUPERIORS WHO ARE COWARDS.
IT FEELS GOOD.
IT FEELS VERY GOOD.

!
HAHA!
HI THERE, MAJOR.
IT'S BEEN A LONG TIME, ALUCARD.
BEING ABLE TO SEE YOU AGAINST THE PINNACLE OF GLADNESS.

?
SO *YOU'RE* THE ENEMY LEADER.

OHH, YOU'RE THE DIRECTOR OF HELLSING.
SIR INTEGRA HELLSING, JA? THIS IST THE FIRST TIME VE'VE MET.
WHAT'S YOUR GOAL?
WHAT LEADS YOU TO ENGAGE IN THIS DAFT BEHAVIOR?
ANSWER ME!!
GOAL?
FRÄULEIN, LOVELY FRÄULEIN. THAT IST ONE FOOLISH QUESTION.
ORDER 23 / END

ORDER 24

GOAL?
HMHM, MY GOAL YOU SAY.
IF YOU MUST GO THAT FAR, FRÄULEIN,
VE DO NOT HAF ANY GOAL.

ORDER 24
ウルテイマ オンライン
ULTIMA ON LINE

HOGWASH!!
H--!
GTAK
!!
YOU MEAN TO SAY YOU ATTACKED US FOR NO REASON?!
EVEN AS A JOKE, THIS...
SILENCE!
DON'T TRY TO TELL US YOU HAVEN'T ANY GOAL!!
IT HAST BEEN SO LONG SINCE I SPOKE VITH A YOUNG GIRL. DO NOT INTERFERE VITH ME, BOY!!
I AM NOT SPEAKING VITH YOU. I AM SPEAKING VITH THIS FRÄULEIN.
I'M TOLD IT'S A MACHIAVELLIAN RUDIMENT, BUT I DON'T REALLY KNOW SUCH THINGS.
SETTLE ON NO MEANS IN OBTAINING YOUR GOALS.
... ...!!
...WHA! ...!!

IN OTHER VORDS...
...TO SETTLE ON NO GOALS IN OBTAINING THEIR MEANS.
DO YOU SEE, FRÄULEIN? IF YOU ARE A COMMANDER VITH THE SLIGHTEST POWER OF RETALIATION, YOU SHOULD KNOW THIS.
THERE IST NO DOUBT THAT IN THIS VORLD, THERE EXIST GROUPS WHO ARE DETERMINED...
KATZ
KATZ
KATZ
KATZ
KATZ
KATZ
Zum Henker defatist!!
Zum H defat
*I AM A DEFEATIST.

HAHAHAHAHAH
SMIRK
GROUPS LIKE US...
AFTER ALL'S SAID UND DONE...
SNAP

RUSH
CRUNCH
...DON'T LEAVE THE JOB HALF FINISHED.
EVEN LETTING HIM BECOME A GHOUL VOULD BE...
BOTHER-SOME.
SHRED
CRACK

UHAHHHH!
THAT LOOKS PRET-TY SEVERE, MAJOR!
DROP
SHIVER

SNAP
RIP
YOU ARE ALL INSANE.
HMMM, YOU SPEAK OF MADNESS TO ME?
VATICAN SECTION XIII CHIEF?
YES, I DO.
NOT ONE OF YOU IS SOUND IN THE MIND.

[opening hand suddenly]

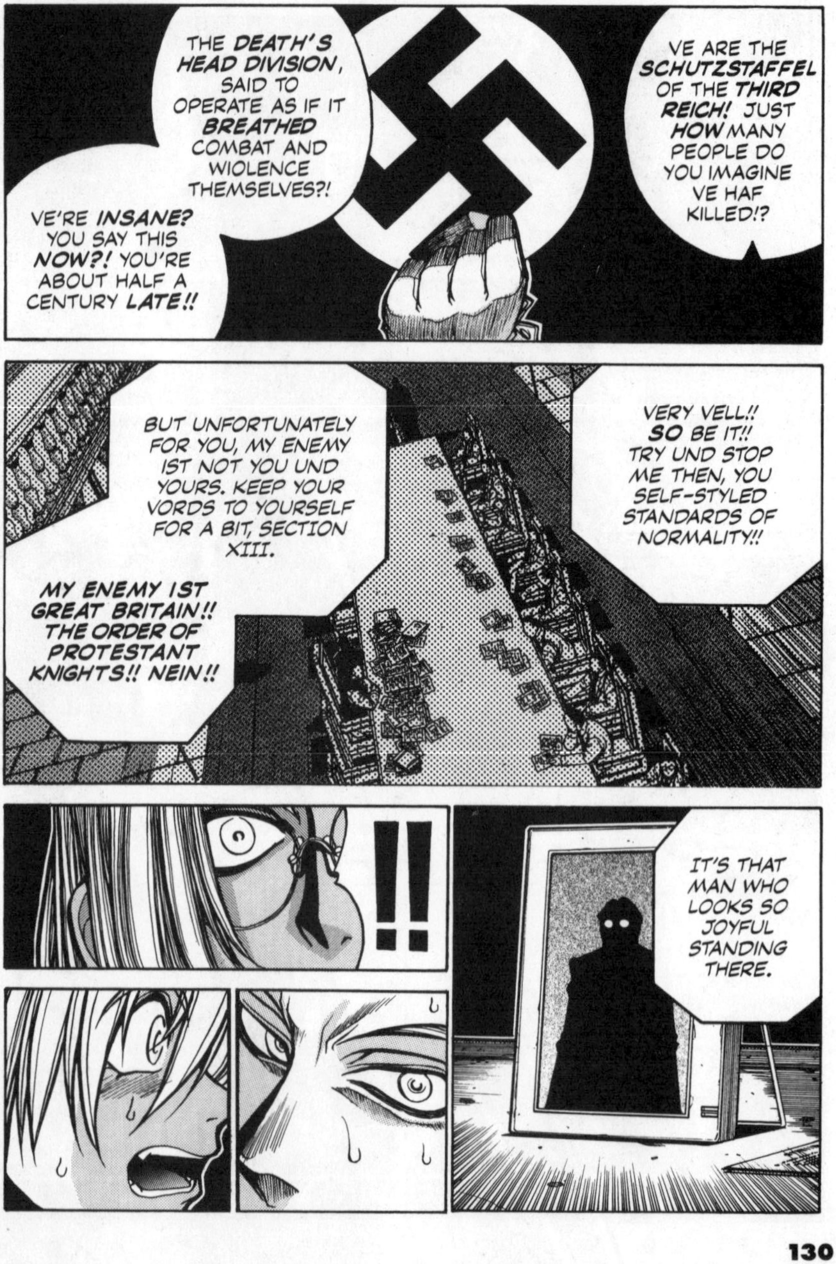
VE ARE THE SCHUTZSTAFFEL OF THE THIRD REICH! JUST HOW MANY PEOPLE DO YOU IMAGINE VE HAF KILLED!?
THE DEATH'S HEAD DIVISION, SAID TO OPERATE AS IF IT BREATHED COMBAT AND WIOLENCE THEMSELVES?!
VE'RE INSANE? YOU SAY THIS NOW?! YOU'RE ABOUT HALF A CENTURY LATE!!
VERY VELL!! SO BE IT!! TRY UND STOP ME THEN, YOU SELF-STYLED STANDARDS OF NORMALITY!!
BUT UNFORTUNATELY FOR YOU, MY ENEMY IST NOT YOU UND YOURS. KEEP YOUR VORDS TO YOURSELF FOR A BIT, SECTION XIII.
MY ENEMY IST GREAT BRITAIN!! THE ORDER OF PROTESTANT KNIGHTS!! NEIN!!
IT'S THAT MAN WHO LOOKS SO JOYFUL STANDING THERE.
!!

TWITCH
TWITCH
TWITCH
HUH HUH HUH HUH HUH HUH!
HUHAH HAHAHA HAHAH!
HAHA HAHA HAHAH!
HAHA HAHA HAHAH!

ALUCARD.
SERAS.
FIRE.
VE'LL OVERTURN UN-SATISFACTORY RESULTS ANY NUMBER OF TIMES.
OF COURSE, VE ARE THE MOST VENGEFUL TYPE THERE IST.
YOU REALLY **ARE** A VENGEFUL BROOD! ***HAHAHAHAH.*** A SUPERB WAR DECLARATION!
FINE, FINE, I'LL DESTROY YOU ANY ***NUMBER*** OF TIMES.

GORP
?!
BLAM
WHMP
!
DEAR ME, SUCH VIOLENT OUTBURSTS.
SHOOTING THE MESSENGER.

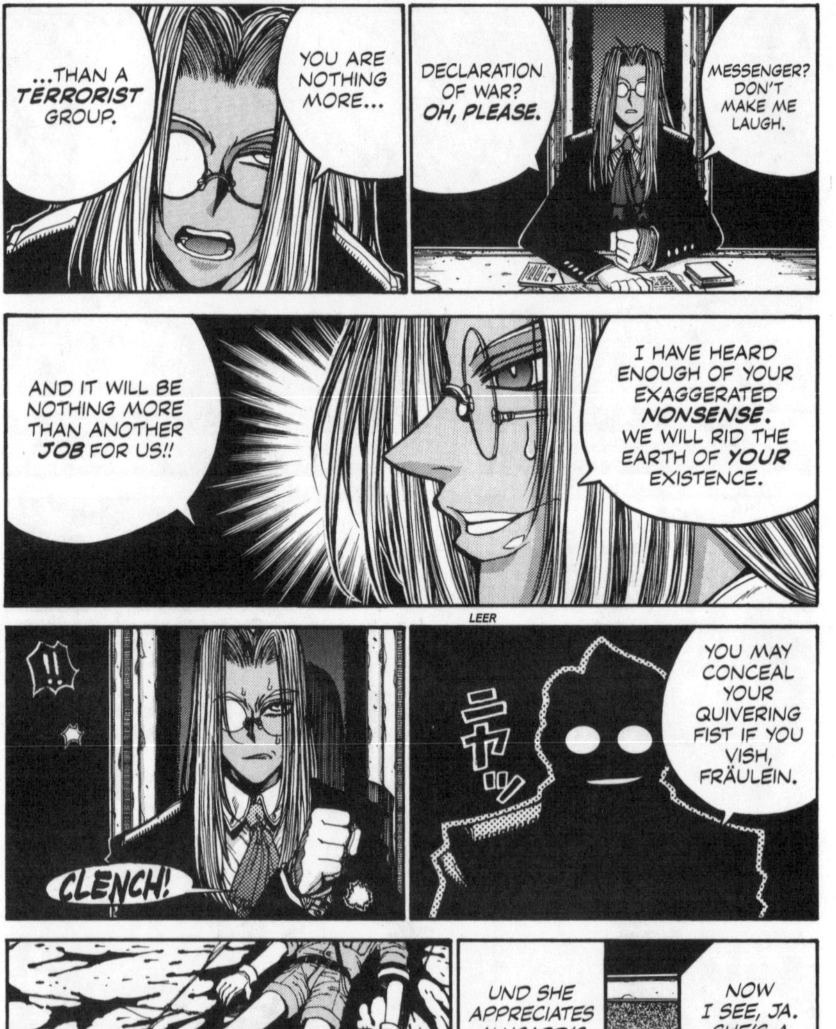

MESSENGER? DON'T MAKE ME LAUGH.
DECLARATION OF WAR? OH, PLEASE.
YOU ARE NOTHING MORE...
...THAN A TERRORIST GROUP.
I HAVE HEARD ENOUGH OF YOUR EXAGGERATED NONSENSE. WE WILL RID THE EARTH OF YOUR EXISTENCE.
AND IT WILL BE NOTHING MORE THAN ANOTHER JOB FOR US!!
LEER
ニヤッ
YOU MAY CONCEAL YOUR QUIVERING FIST IF YOU VISH, FRÄULEIN.
!!
CLENCH!
NOW I SEE, JA. SHE'S A GOOD MASTER.
UND SHE APPRECIATES ALUCARD'S EFFORTS.

!!
FAREVELL, FRÄULEIN.
I LOOK FORWARD TO MEETING YOU AGAIN ON THE FIELD OF BATTLE.
AUF WIEDERSEHEN!
SERAS!!
BKOOM
HAH!
ROGER!!
HAH!
HAH!

SIR HELLSING.
ALUCARD.
THIS IS AN ORDER.
BRING THEM ALL DOWN.
ORDER 24 / END

ORDER 25

INTELLIGENCE SEEMS TAE BE LEAKING TAE THEM LIKE IT WAS KEPT IN AE *SIEVE*.
AYE, AH WIDNAE DOUBT IT.
AS WE RECKONED, THEIR ARM'S AE LANG YIN.
AH'VE ALREADY BEEN ATTACKED FOOR TIMES SINCE AH GOT T' THIS CONTINENT.

AH RUN INTO YIN O' THESE DAMNED VAMPIRE ADHERENTS EFTER THE NEXT.
BUT WHIT AH DINNAE UNDERSTAND IS WHY THEY HAVE NAE SENT YIN "VAMPIRE" OOT EFTER ME.
LIKE AH'M BEING MADE FUN O'.
MAXWELL, THINGS HAVE PROCEEDED ACCORDING TAE YER PLANS.
THEIR TARGET IS BRITAIN. HMPH.
ARENAE YE BURSTING WI' JOY?
HALF OF ME IS. HOWEVER...
THE OTHER HALF IS QUITE DISPLEASED!!
THEY ARE TRYING TO KEEP YOU OCCUPIED, BUY THEMSELVES TIME.
PROBABLY. THE QUESTION IS...
...WHIT ARE A' YON VAMPIRES UP TAE?

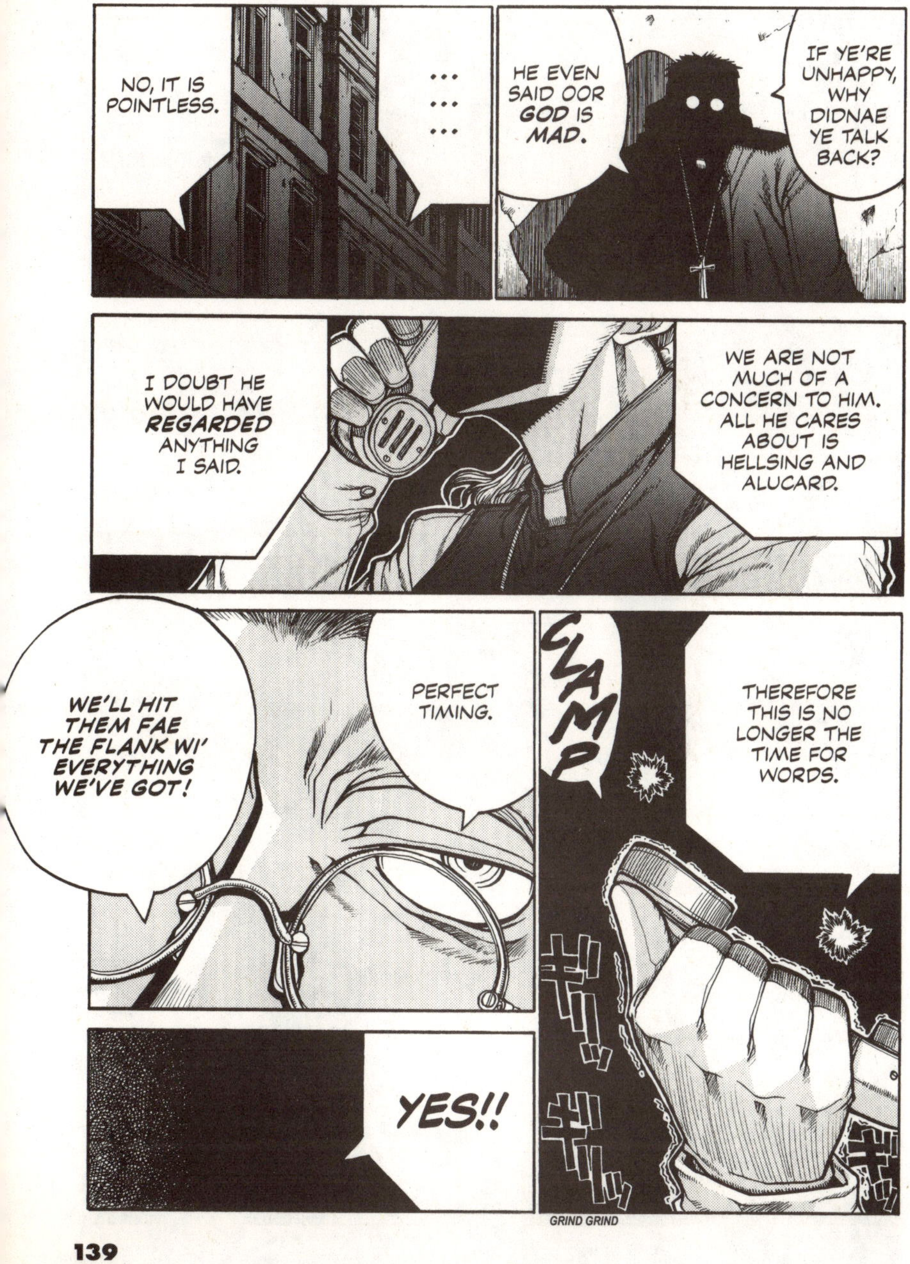
IF YE'RE UNHAPPY, WHY DIDNAE YE TALK BACK?
HE EVEN SAID OOR GOD IS MAD.
...
...
...
NO, IT IS POINTLESS.
WE ARE NOT MUCH OF A CONCERN TO HIM. ALL HE CARES ABOUT IS HELLSING AND ALUCARD.
I DOUBT HE WOULD HAVE REGARDED ANYTHING I SAID.
THEREFORE THIS IS NO LONGER THE TIME FOR WORDS.
CLAMP
PERFECT TIMING.
WE'LL HIT THEM FAE THE FLANK WI' EVERYTHING WE'VE GOT!
YES!!
GRIND GRIND

HOO?
A LITTLE WHILE AGO, MOBILIZATION ORDERS CAME THROUGH FROM HIS HOLINESS.
AT THE END OF ALL THINGS, IT WILL BE US STANDING IN THE RING WITH OUR FISTS RAISED.
OUR HOLY RELIC ADMINISTRATION BUREAU, SECTION III "MATTHEW," IS ALSO IN MOTION. THEY ARE PREPARING WEAPONS THOUGHT TO BE SUITED FOR ANTI-VAMPIRE COMBAT.
I HAVE SHIFTED THE HEADQUARTERS OF THE KNIGHTS OF MALTA, THE ORDER OF ST. JOHN, THE HOSPITALLERS, THE ORDER OF ST. GEORGE...
...AS WELL AS THE SWISS GUARD TO THIS PLACE.
YES. UNDENIABLY. BUT OUR ENEMY IS NOT ALLAH.
HUHUHUH. THON MEANS WE'RE JUST LIKE CRUSADERS.
IT IS FITTING, AFTER ALL. WE SHALL PILE THEIR CORPSES UP FROM EVERY HIGH WALL TO EVERY STREET CORNER JUST AS WE DID ONCE BEFORE.
THE GOD THIS TIME IS MARS.

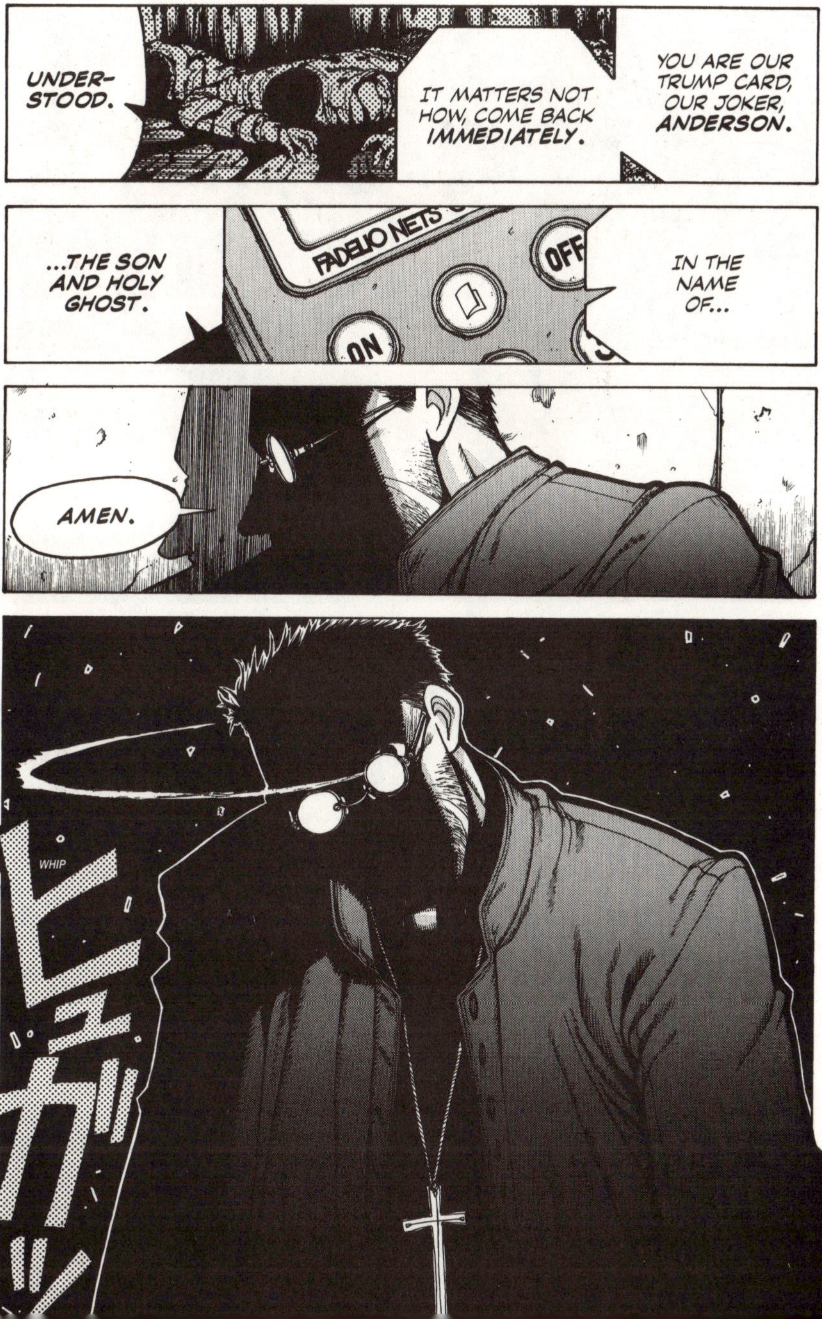

YOU ARE OUR TRUMP CARD, OUR JOKER, **ANDERSON**.
IT MATTERS NOT HOW, COME BACK **IMMEDIATELY**.
UNDER-STOOD.
IN THE NAME OF...
...THE SON AND HOLY GHOST.
FADELIO NETS
OFF
ON
AMEN.
WHIP
ヒュガッ

!!
!!
WHIT DAE YE THINK...
...YE CAN DAE TAE ME WI YON TOYS?
ZFF
ZPP
TMP
TMP
TMP
TMP
TMP
TMP

DO DO DO DO DO DO DO
ドドドドドドド
ガーンガーンガーンガーン
BLAM BLAM BLAM BLAM
SSS!

SHNK
SHNK
SHANK
MARS, MARS, MARS!!
A' RICHT THEN, YE BITCH! WE'LL GIE YE AE GUID TASTE O' OOR DIVINE PUNISHMENT!

⚜ ORDER 25

——D①——

(ディー)

THERE IST NO GOING BACK NOW.
KATZ KATZ KATZ KATZ KATZ KATZ KATZ
VAT ARE YOU SAYING? THE CURTAIN HAS BEEN UP ON THIS PLAY FOR OVER FIFTY YEARS.
IT'S JUST THAT THE AUDIENCE HASN'T BEEN LOOKING THIS VAY.
KATZ KATZ KATZ KATZ KATZ KATZ
VE'VE GRABBED THEM BY THE SCRUFF OF THEIR NECKS UND TURNED THEIR EYES TO US.
UND VONCE THE DANCE BEGINS, I VILL DANCE UNTIL THE VERY END.
AS MUCH FUN AS CAN BE.
KATZ KATZ KATZ
...
...

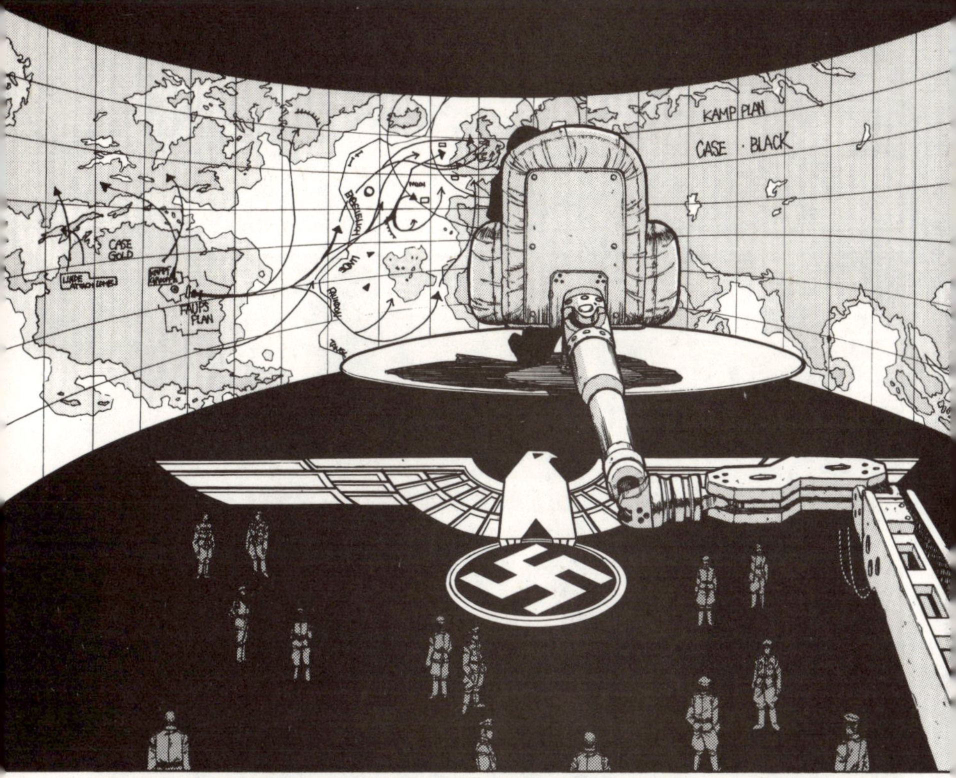
KAMP PLAN
CASE · BLACK
CASE GOLD

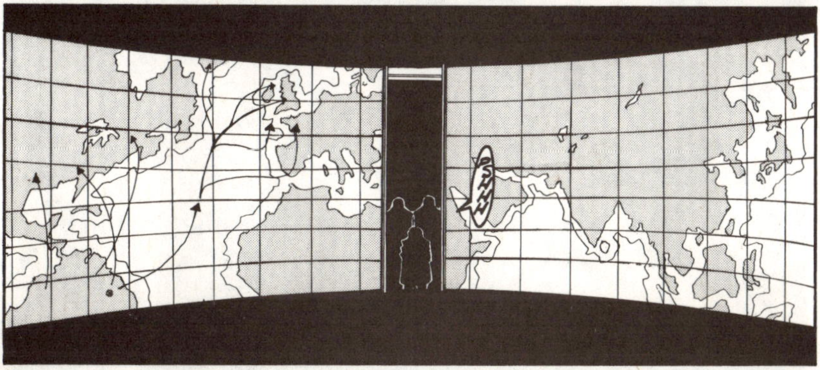
SHHH

KATZ
KATZ
KATZ
KATZ
KATZ
SHF
SHF
SHFA
SUWAP!
YOU'RE SLOWWW.
!
?!

IN THE TIME IT TOOK YOU TO VALK DOWN THE HALLVAY...
...I VENT ALL THE VAY TO LONDON, HAD A FREAKISHLY HUGE GUN GO OFF IN MY MOUTH...
GOT MY HEAD BLOWN OFF, UND CAME BACK HOME.
VNNN
VOULDN'T IT BE A GOOD IDEA TO GO ON A DIET?
MAJORRR.
HAHAHA.
I'M AFRAID THAT'S IMPOSSIBLE.
ZSHHH

GRAB
YANK
VARRANT OFFICER SCHRÖDINGER.
DIDN'T I TELL YOU TO STOP BEING RUDE?!
IT'S OKAY, DOK. IT'S OKAY.
THE CHIEF CARRIED OUT HIS MISSION.
JA, BUT --!!
NO MATTER. LET HIM DO AS HE VANTS.
......!!
KNEEL

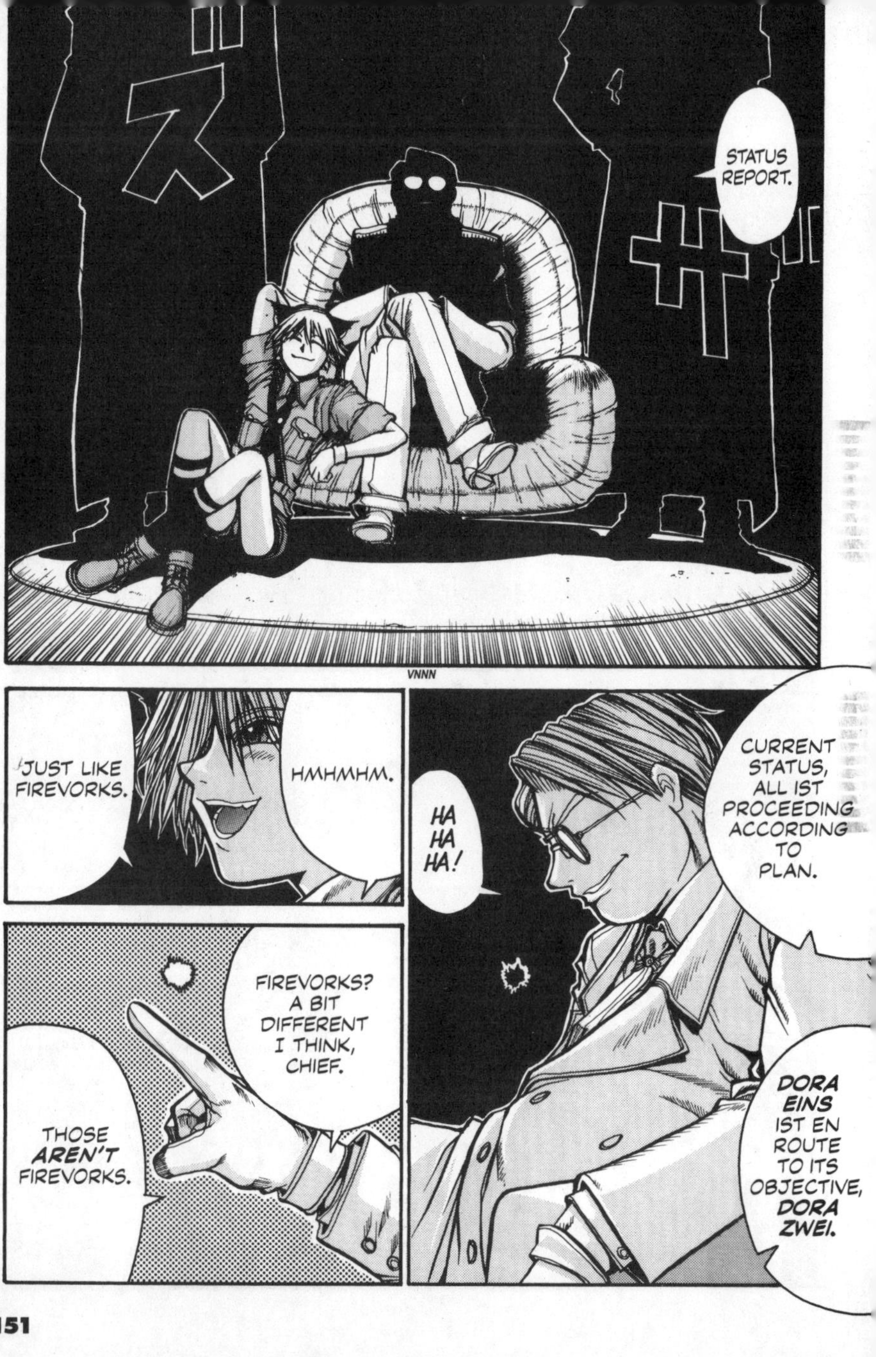
STATUS REPORT.
VNNN
CURRENT STATUS, ALL IST PROCEEDING ACCORDING TO PLAN.
HA HA HA!
HMHMHM.
JUST LIKE FIREVORKS.
DORA EINS IST EN ROUTE TO ITS OBJECTIVE, DORA ZWEI.
FIREVORKS? A BIT DIFFERENT I THINK, CHIEF.
THOSE AREN'T FIREVORKS.

THEY'RE BEACONS.
BEACONS OF TREACHERY TO SHOW THE VORLD THAT VE HAF RETURNED TO IT.
GYOOOO
BADDA BADDA BADDA BADDA BADDA BADDA
BADDA BADDA BADDA BADDA

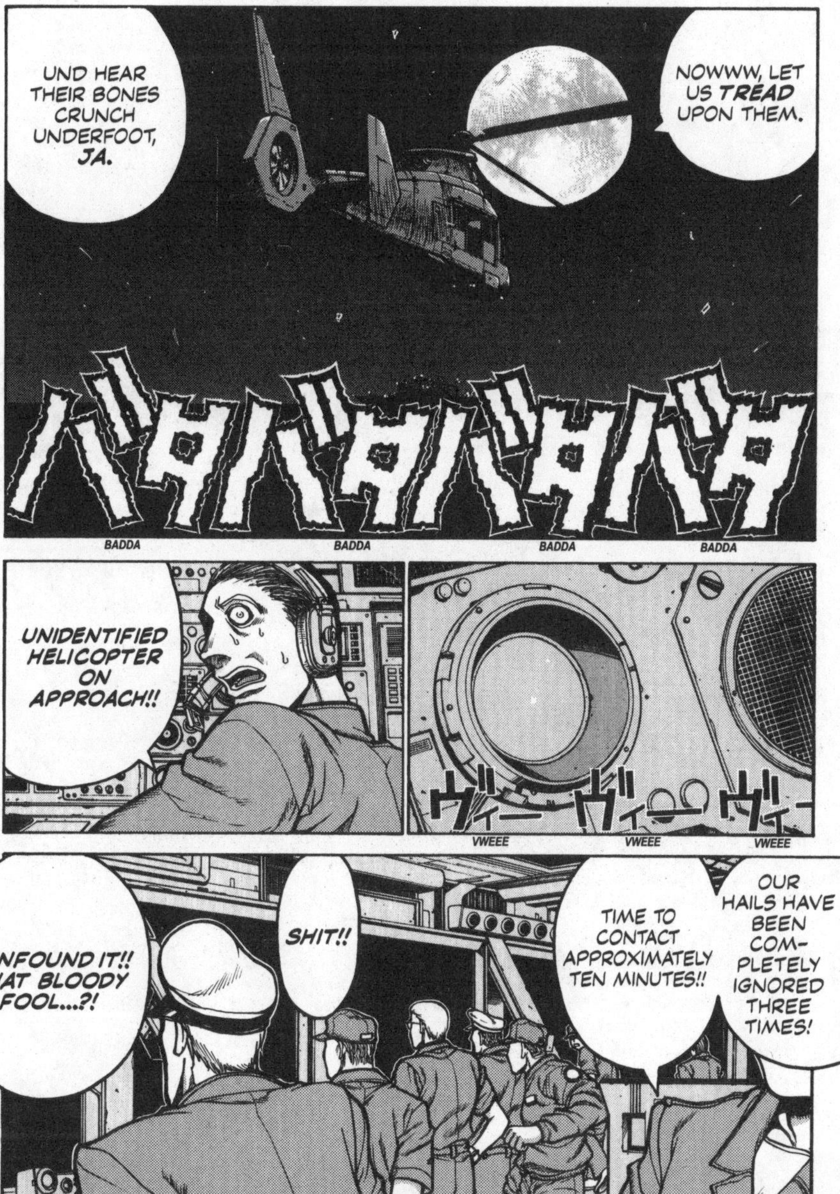
NOWWW, LET US TREAD UPON THEM.
UND HEAR THEIR BONES CRUNCH UNDERFOOT, JA.
バタバタバタバタ
BADDA BADDA BADDA BADDA
ヴィー ヴィー ヴィー
VWEEE VWEEE VWEEE
UNIDENTIFIED HELICOPTER ON APPROACH!!
OUR HAILS HAVE BEEN COMPLETELY IGNORED THREE TIMES!
TIME TO CONTACT APPROXIMATELY TEN MINUTES!!
SHIT!!
CONFOUND IT!! WHAT BLOODY FOOL...?!

DENN WIR FAHREN.
"WE ARE DRIVING ON."
BRITISH ROYAL NAVY INVINCIBLE CLASS VSTOL AIRCRAFT CARRIER FLAGSHIP HMS EAGLE.
GEGEN ENGLAND!
"AGAINST ENGLAND!
AUF NACH ENGLAND!
OFF TO ENGLAND!"
ORDER 25 / END

ORDER 26

DENN WIR WOLLEN ES NICHT
"WE DON'T WANT TO
LÄNGER ERLEIDEN.
SUFFER ANY LONGER."
BADDA BADDA BADDA
WIR LACHEN DIE ENGLÄNDER
"WE LAUGH AT THE ENGLISH
AUS WÄHREND WIR ANGREIFEN.
AS WE GO TO INVADE."
DENN WIR FAHREN...
"WE ARE DRIVING ON,"
BADDA BADDA BADDA
DENN WIR FAHREN,
"WE ARE DRIVING ON,"
GEGEN ENGLAND!
"AGAINST ENGLAND!
AUF NACH ENGLAND!
OFF TO ENGLAND!"

ORDER 26
ディー
D②

UNIDENTIFIED HELICOPTER APPROACHING THE SHIP!!
RUBBISH!! THEY MUST BE OUT OF THEIR MINDS!
WHO THE BLOODY HELL?!
OUR WARNINGS HAVE BEEN COMPLETELY IGNORED THREE TIMES!
IT WON'T BE LONG BEFORE IT REACHES US!!
CAPTAIN!!
...
...
THERE'S NOTHING FOR IT!!
PREPARE A WARNING SHOT WITH THE CIWS!!
IF THEY IGNORE THAT...
...WE'VE NO OPTION BUT TO SHOOT IT DOWN.
THAT ISN'T GOING TO HAPPEN.
?!
NUMBER ONE?!
WHAT THE HELL ARE YOU...
I'M SAYING I CAN'T ALLOW YOU TO DO THAT.

TOK
Sieg Heil!!
HYUU
LUNGE
SHRIP

SPASHH
WHA A!!
AH... UWA...
!!
SPOSHH
KHAA
AAAAAAAAAAH
GAAAAAAAAAAAAAAA

AAAAAAAAAAAAAAAAAAAGH!
GIB MIR DEINE HAND, "GIVE ME YOUR HAND, DEINE WEIBE HAND. YOUR WHITE HAND.
TWITCH
LEB' WOHL MEIN SCHATZ, "GOOD-BYE MY LOVE, LEB' WOHL. GOOD-BYE.
TWITCH
SELBST "EVEN IF WORD WENN DIE KUNDE COMES THAT KOMMT DAB ICH I'VE FALLEN IN GEFALLEN BIN, BATTLE,
DAB ICH SCHLAFE IN "AND AM SLEEPING IN THE DER MEERESFLUT, DEPTHS OF THE SEA,

WEINE NICHT UM MICH, "DON'T CRY FOR ME, MEIN SCHATZ. MY LOVE.
DENN WIR FAHREN, "WE ARE DRIVING ON,
DENN WIR FAHREN, "WE ARE DRIVING ON,
GEGEN ENGLAND! "AGAINST ENGLAND! AUF NACH ENGLAND! OFF TO ENGLAND!
DENN WIR FAHREN. "WE ARE DRIVING ON."

BADDA
BADDA
BADDA
SHMM
KATZ
SHMM
SHMM

THUS THE HUNTING GROUND BECOMES THE HUNTER'S.
UND MY VARHEAD VILL PUNISH ALL VITHOUT DISTINCTION.

プル・ プル..
SHUDDER
SHUDDER

SLRP...
CLAMP
GEH!
KHOF!
GHOF!
ULP!
...
...!
UBB!
...
...!
HNG!
GULP!
...
...
HAHH.
HAHH.
HAH!
HAHH.

IS IT PAINFUL?
HAI
IT MUST BE.
CHIEF...!!
MEDICAL BLOOD
DOMM
!!

I HEARD FROM WALTER.
THIS IS THE WAY YOU'VE BEEN AT MEALTIME LATELY.
WHY DON'T YOU DRINK IT?
THE BLOOD.
YOU AREN'T HUMAN ANYMORE. YOU ARE A VAMPIRE, SERAS.
BUT...! I... ...
I MEAN... ...!
THAT IS... UH...
...
...!
?!
KATZ
KATZ
KATZ
REACH

!
!!
DRIP
PLIP
?!
GTUNK
M--!
M--!
MISS INTEGRA!!
LOOOM
I'VE CUT MY FINGER.
AT THIS RATE IT MIGHT GET INFECTED.
LICK IT FOR ME.
EH!
WAHH
AH!
ER, EH?!

...BOUND TO MY ORDERS, SERAS?
ARE YOU NOT...
THAT'S AN ORDER.
LICK IT.
......
AH!
HAH.
......
HA!
HAH.
......
......
AH!
......
AH!
DON'T FORGET YOURSELF AND BITE DOWN, ALL RIGHT?
BE MINDFUL, SERAS.
......
HAH.

ぷぱっ
SHLLP
THE GENUINE ARTICLE, **100% VIRGIN BLOOD.**
DID IT RELIEVE YOU SOMEWHAT, POLICE GIRL?
UH... AH...
WELL... I...
TH... THANK... YOU...
ダラダラ
DUH DUH
だ―
DUHHHHHH
ダラダラ
DUH DUH
PREPARE YOUR GEAR AND STAND BY, **POLICE GIRL!!**
カッ
KATZ
COMMUNICATION WAS LOST WITH THE ***HMS EAGLE*** SOMEWHERE AT SEA NEAR WALES.
LIKELY DUE TO **MILLENNIUM.**
カッ
KATZ
カッ
KATZ
R-RIGHT.
Y--!
YAHHHH!!

ORDER 26 / END

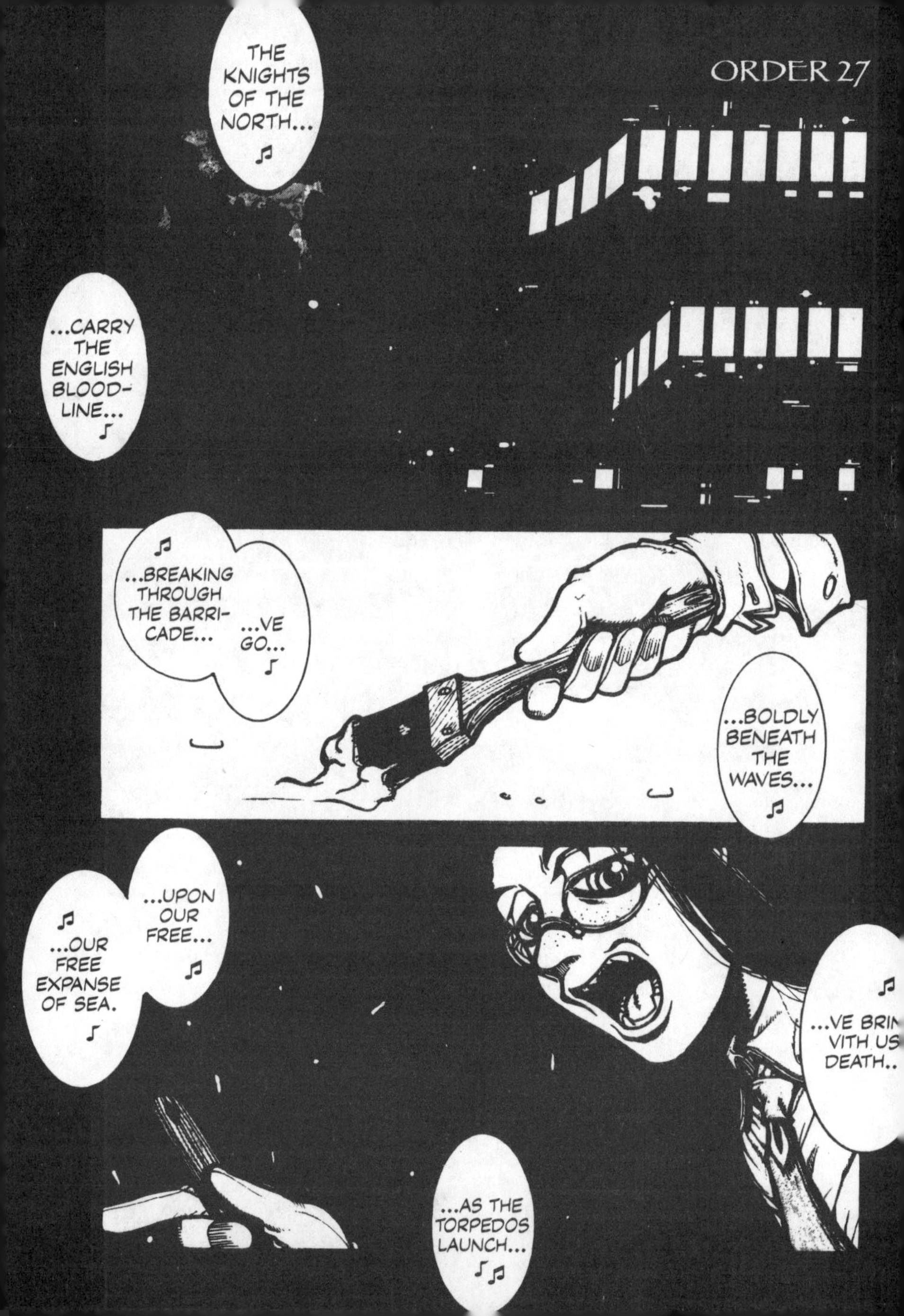
ORDER 27
THE KNIGHTS OF THE NORTH... ♫
...CARRY THE ENGLISH BLOODLINE... ♪
♫ ...BREAKING THROUGH THE BARRICADE...
...VE GO... ♪
...BOLDLY BENEATH THE WAVES... ♫
...UPON OUR FREE... ♫
♫ ...OUR FREE EXPANSE OF SEA. ♪
♫ ...VE BRIN VITH US DEATH..
...AS THE TORPEDOS LAUNCH... ♪♫

ORDER 27
D③ (ディー)

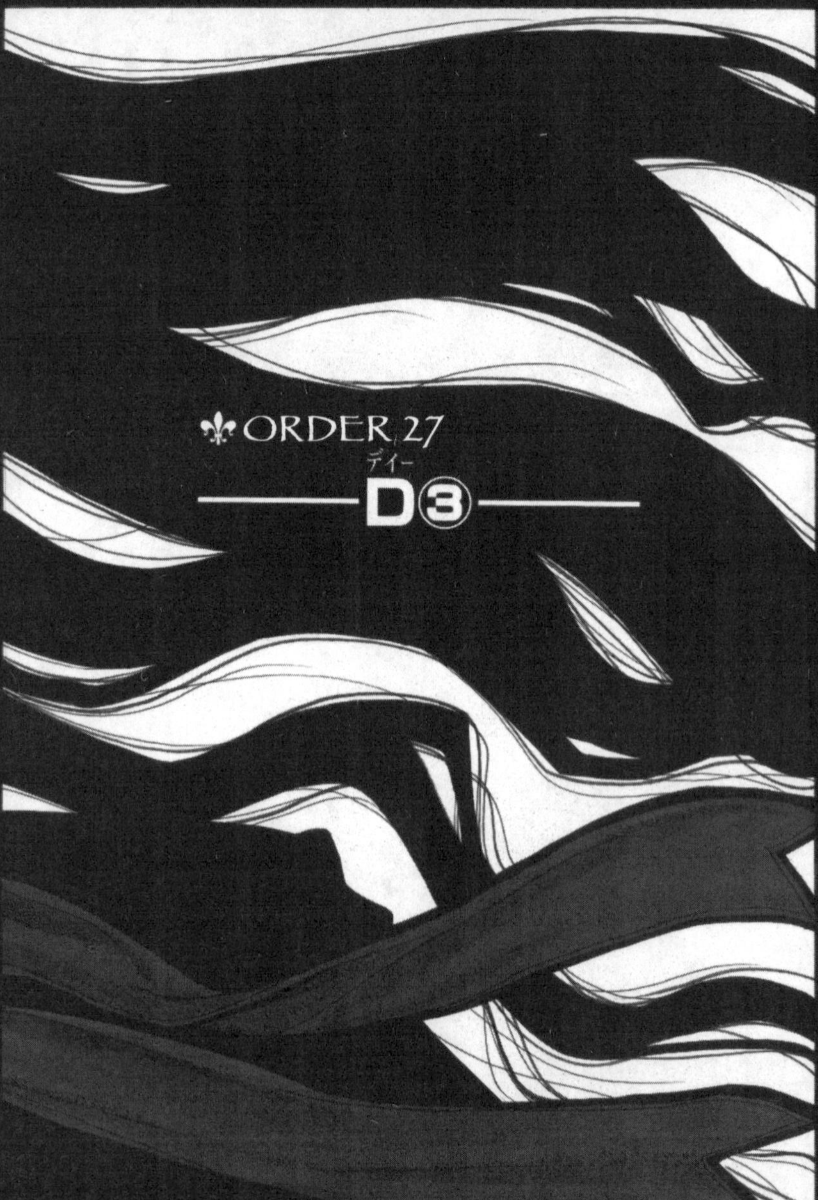

WELCOME!!
WELCOME TO OUR SHIP!!
JUST AS YOU WISHED, BOTH WE AND OUR SHIP...
...HAVE JOINED WITH MILLEN-NIUM!!
VAT ARE YOUR THOUGHTS ON BEING A VAMPIRE, "NUMBER VONE?"
IT'S SMASHING!
WONDERFUL!! WONDERFUL!!
SO THIS, THIS IS WHAT IT MEANS TO BE A VAMPIRE!!
I SEE.
THAT'S GOOD FOR YOU.

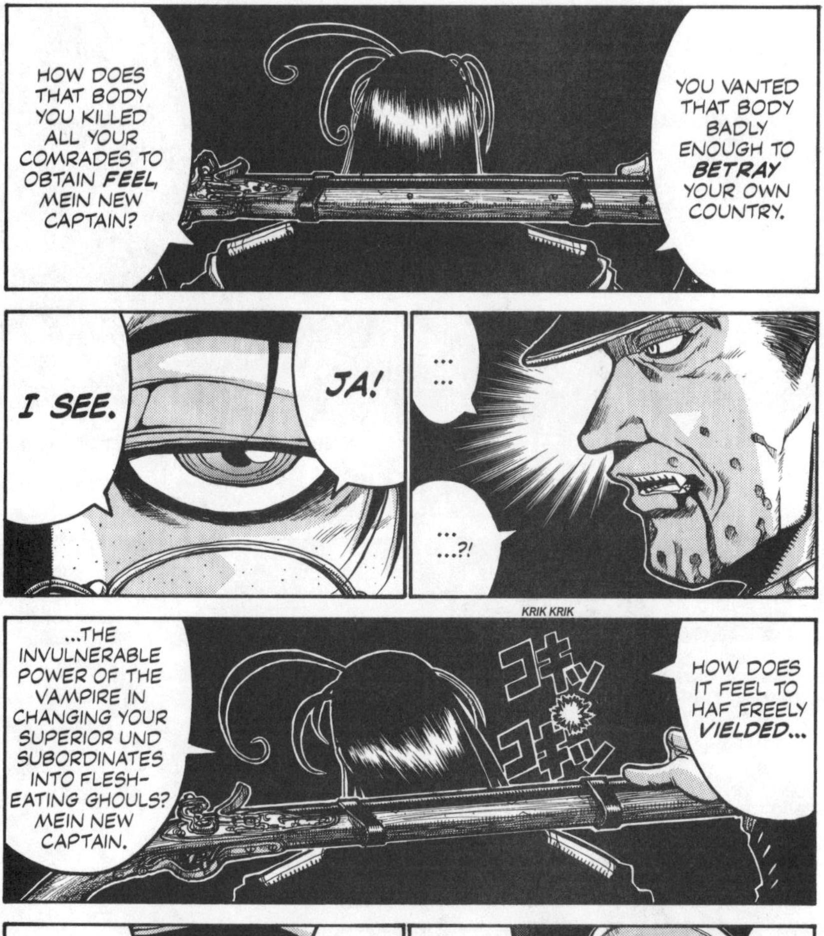
HOW DOES THAT BODY YOU KILLED ALL YOUR COMRADES TO OBTAIN *FEEL*, MEIN NEW CAPTAIN?
YOU VANTED THAT BODY BADLY ENOUGH TO *BETRAY* YOUR OWN COUNTRY.
I SEE.
JA!
... ...
... ...?!
KRIK KRIK
...THE INVULNERABLE POWER OF THE VAMPIRE IN CHANGING YOUR SUPERIOR UND SUBORDINATES INTO FLESH-EATING GHOULS? MEIN NEW CAPTAIN.
HOW DOES IT FEEL TO HAF FREELY *VIELDED*...
I SEE.
JA!
... ...?!
... WHA...
TWITCH
TWITCH
TWITCH

VELL DONE!! VUNDER-BAR!! VAT A FANTASTIC JOB.
VE OF MILLENNIUM EXTEND TO YOU A WERY VARM VELCOME!!
TURN
NEIN, THIS REALLY IST A GREAT ACHIEVEMENT. THE PLAN VOULDN'T HAVE VORKED IF NOT FOR YOU.
OUR KOMMANDANT, DER FÜHRER, IS ALSO VERY VERY PLEASED!!
...NOW CONCERNING YOUR MOST EXCELLENT REVARD...
UND YOUR NEWLY ISSUED ORDERS.
UMM... I BELIEVE... JAAA.
IT'S TO PRESENT YOURSELVES AS PERMANENT ADDITIONS...
...TO A TWO MILE CUBIC AREA IN THE OCEAN IN ALL DIRECTIONS FROM THIS POINT!!
SMILE
EH...?!
REGARDING YOUR NEW ORDERS.
THE SPRINKLING OF FOOD IN THIS VICINITY OF THE OCEAN TO PROVIDE NUTRIENTS FOR THE FISH!!

JUST ONE MINUTE!
WHAT THE HELL'S THAT ALL ABOUT THEN?!
OH, MY.
GRIND
GRIND
GNASH GRIND
MAYBE THAT VAS A BIT HARD TO GRASP.
I'LL SAY IT SIMPLER SO EVEN STUPID PUPS LIKE YOU CAN UNDERSTAND.
THE JOB'S DONE, NOW BE A GOOD BOY UND DIE.
DIRTY LIMEY.

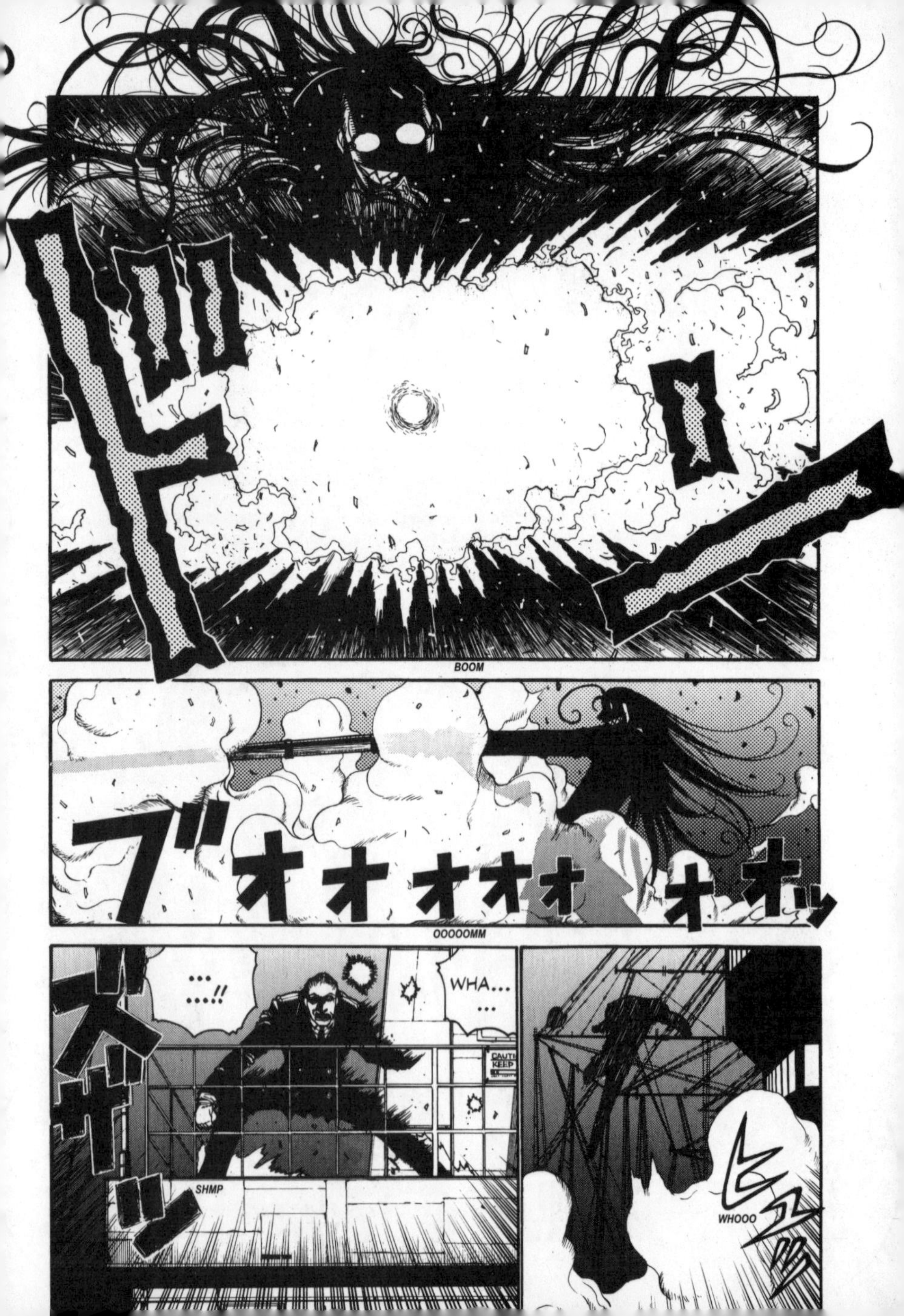
BOOM
ブオオオオオオオッ
OOOOOMM
WHOOO
WHA...
...
...
....!!
SHMP

YOU!
YOU TRICKED ME, YOU BITCH!!
!!
SWAY
WHUMP
THLP
WHUMP
SHLUMP
WH--A?!
HOW COULD... ...THAT?!
THERE WAS ONLY ONE GUNSHOT!!
CHAK
IMPOSSIBLE ...!!
THAT'S IMPOSSIBLE!!
I AM THE HUNTRESS RIP VAN WINKLE.
MY VARHEAD VILL PUNISH ALL VITHOUT DISTINCTION.

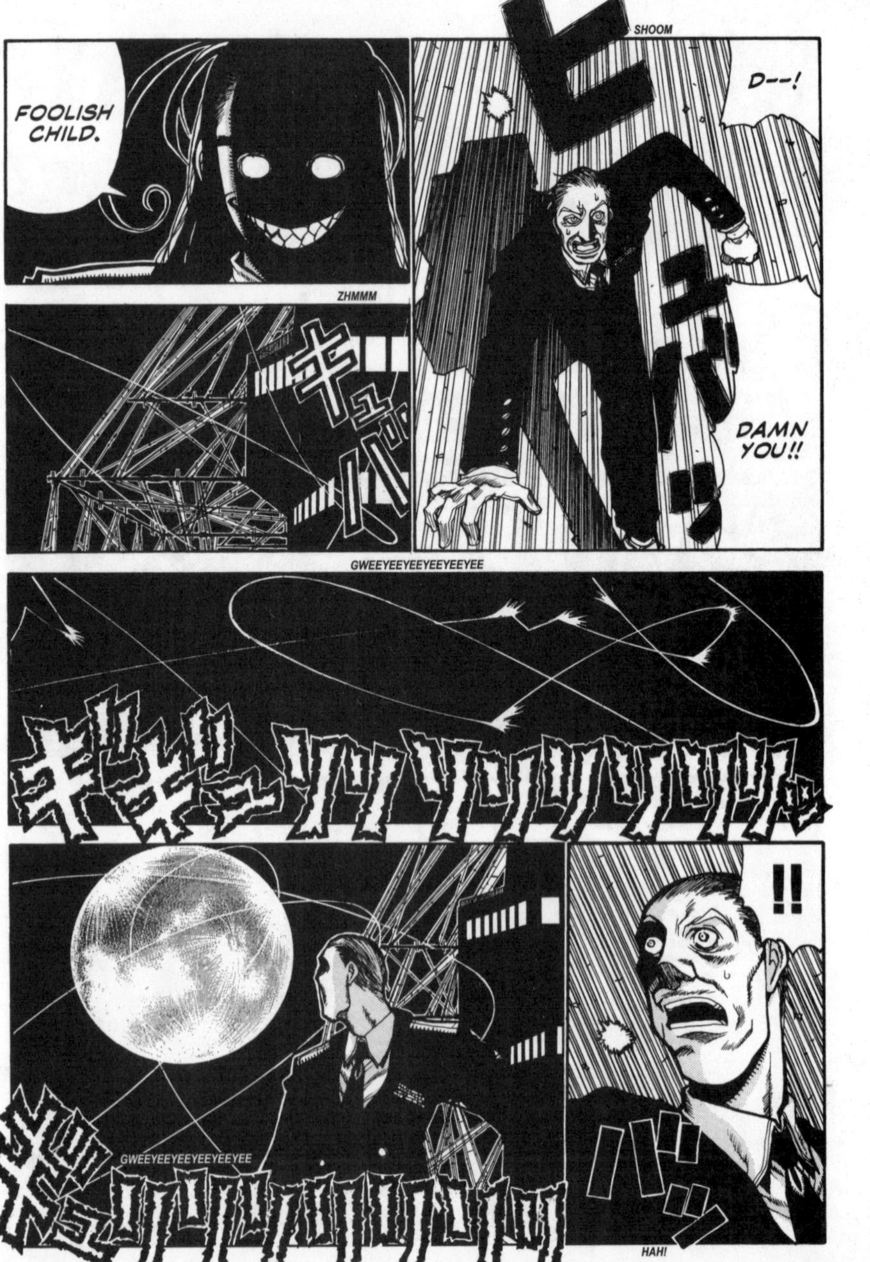
SHOOM
D--!
DAMN YOU!!
FOOLISH CHILD.
ZHMMM
GWEEYEEYEEYEEYEEYEE
!!
HAH!
GWEEYEEYEEYEEYEEYEE

VREEEEEE
OHHHH!
HEE...
BKOK
THNK

THUMP
THUMP
DKUNK
ドカッ
DKUNK
ドガッ
DKUNK
ドガッ
SHFF
ぞろ
SHFF
ぞろ
SHFF
ぞろッ

KRIK☆
!!
!
♫
♫
ヒュオオオオオ
WHOOOOO

ズル
ズッ
SHLP SHLP
SHLP SHLP
LIEUTENANT.
AH.
YOU'RE AVAKE?
SMILE
DMP
THE PAINT RAN OUT HALFVAY THROUGH...
BUT I MANAGED.
YOU KNOW, VITHOUT **THIS,**
THERE'S JUST NO **SENSE** THAT THE SHIP IST OURS.

BEARING OUR ACCURSED NATIONAL STANDARD...
THE *ADLER*, NAVAL FLAGSHIP OF THE...
...GERMAN THIRD REICH'S ATLANTIC FLEET, HEREBY MOBILIZES UND BEGINS ITS *MISSION!!*

GENTLEMEN,
I LOVE VAR.
GENTLEMEN, I...
...LOVE VAR.
GENTLEMEN.
I SO LOVE VAR.

I LOVE BESIEGEMENT. I LOVE BREAKTHROUGH. I LOVE RETREAT. I LOVE MOP-UP. I LOVE VITHDRAWAL.
I LOVE HOLOCAUST. I LOVE BLITZKRIEG. I LOVE ONSLAUGHT. I LOVE DEFENSIVE.
ON THE PLAINS, IN THE STREETS, IN THE TRENCHES, ON THE PRAIRIES, ON THE TUNDRA, IN THE DESERT, ON THE SEA, IN THE SKY, IN THE MUD, IN THE SVAMP.
I CHERISH EACH UND EVERY VAY VAR CAN BE VAGED ON THIS EARTH.

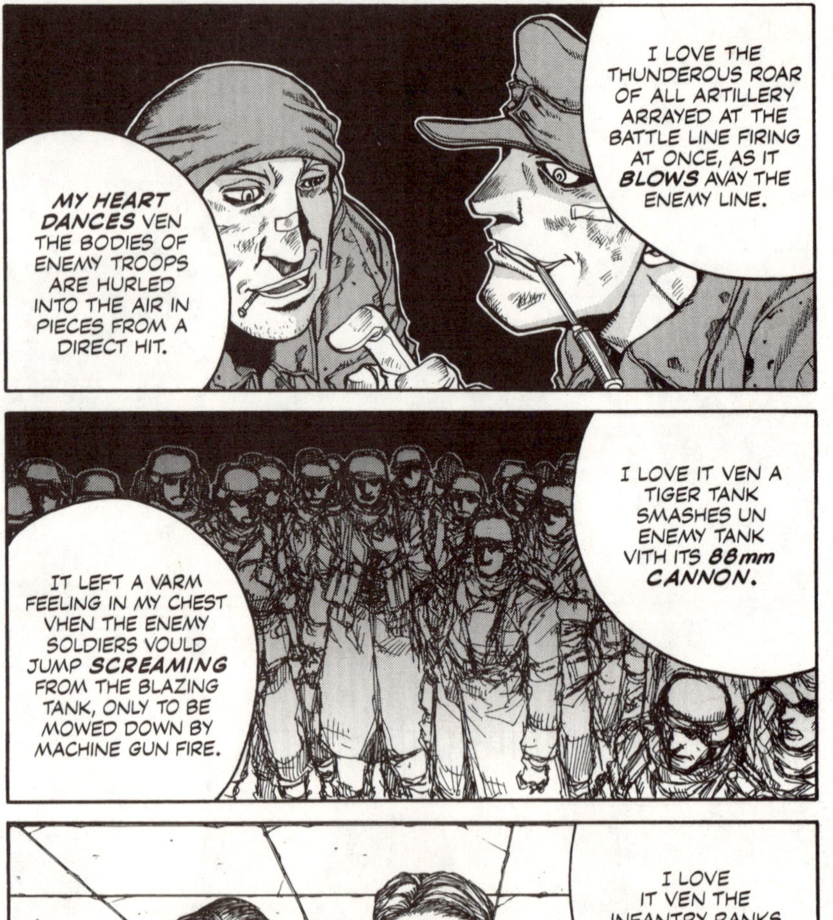

I LOVE THE THUNDEROUS ROAR OF ALL ARTILLERY ARRAYED AT THE BATTLE LINE FIRING AT ONCE, AS IT **BLOWS** AVAY THE ENEMY LINE.
MY HEART DANCES VEN THE BODIES OF ENEMY TROOPS ARE HURLED INTO THE AIR IN PIECES FROM A DIRECT HIT.
I LOVE IT VEN A TIGER TANK SMASHES UN ENEMY TANK VITH ITS **88mm CANNON.**
IT LEFT A VARM FEELING IN MY CHEST VHEN THE ENEMY SOLDIERS VOULD JUMP **SCREAMING** FROM THE BLAZING TANK, ONLY TO BE MOWED DOWN BY MACHINE GUN FIRE.
I LOVE IT VEN THE INFANTRY RANKS **OVERRUN** THE ENEMY LINE, BAYONETS FIRST.
IT MOVES ME VEN I REMEMBER THE SIGHT OF A NEW RECRUIT IN A STATE OF PANIC, STABBING UN ALREADY DEAD ENEMY SOLDIER **OVER UND OVER.**

*NOTE: "80cm RAILWAY CANNON."

*NOTE: SHORT FOR "JAGDBOMBER." WARPLANE FOR ATTACKING ENGLAND AND AMERICA.

GENTLEMEN.
I VISH TO SEE A VAR VORTHY OF ONE IN HELL ITSELF.
GENTLEMEN, MY BATTALION OF COMRADES WHO FOLLOW ME...
PRAY TELL, VAT DO YOU VISH FOR?
DO YOU VISH FOR VAR AS A MATTER OF COURSE?
DO YOU VISH FOR A MERCILESS, SHITLIKE VAR?
DO YOU VISH FOR A STORMLIKE CONFLICT VICH RUNS THE GAMUT OF BLOWING STEEL UND STRIKING FLAME, KILLING EVERY CROW IN THE ENTIRE VORLD?

GA GA GA GA GA GA GA GA
KRIEG!!
KRIEG!!
KRIEG!!
VERY VELL.
THEN LET IT BE KRIEG.

BUT FOR VE WHO HAF CONTINUED TO ENDURE A WHOLE HALF CENTURY IN THE DEPTHS OF THESE DARK SHADOWS...
...A SIMPLE VAR IS NO LONGER ENOUGH!!
ALL OUR STRENGTH IST HELD IN A CLENCHED FIST, POISED TO STRIKE.
CLENCH
SHRNK
ONE BORN OF OUR SINGLE-HEARTED DEVOTION!!
A GREAT VAR!!
BUT I BELIEVE THAT YOU ARE ALL MATCHLESS, HARDENED VETERANS.
VE ARE MERELY ONE BATTALION, NO MORE THAN A THOUSAND TROOP REMNANTS.
SO, GENTLEMEN, TOGETHER VE ARE UN ARMY AS POWERFUL AS A MILLION REGULAR SOLDIERS.

LET US SEIZE THEM BY THEIR HAIR, DRAG THEM DOWN, OPEN THEIR EYES, UND MAKE THEM REMEMBER.
LET US ROUSE THOSE SLUMBERING ONES WHO DROVE US INTO THE REALM OF FORGET-FULNESS.
VE SHALL MAKE THEM REMEMBER THE SOUND OF OUR VAR BOOTS.
VE SHALL MAKE THEM REMEMBER THE TASTE OF TERROR.

VE SHALL REMIND THEM THAT SOMETHING IN THE INTERVAL BETWEEN HEAVEN UND EARTH THEY DON'T EVEN RECALL VITH THEIR PHILOSOPHY DOES INDEED EXIST.
GRAFZEPPELIN III

ゴーンゴーンゴーンゴーン
KONG
GONG
GONG
GONG

GOGOGOGOGOGOGOGOGOGO
THE KAMPF GRUPPE* OF A THOUSAND WAMPIRES...
*NOTE: "KAMPF GRUPPE" IS "BATTLE GROUP."
...VILL BURN THE VORLD TO A CRISP.
GOGOGOGOGOGOGO

GOGOGOGOGOGOGOGO
GOGOGOGOGOGOGOGO
THIS IST *KOMMANDANT* OF THE *LETZTES BATAILLON*, TO THE ENTIRE AIR FLEET.

COMMENCE OPERATION OF ALL FLAPS.
FLAGSHIP **DEUS EX MACHINA** STARTING UP.
RISE!!
RELEASE ALL VIRES UND RESTRAINING CORDS.
GOGOGOGO
OUR OBJECTIVE IST THE SKIES OVER THE BRITISH MAINLAND CAPITOL, **LONDON!!**
GRAF ZEPPELIN III

COMMENCE PREPARATION FOR...
...OPERATION SEE LION 2.
LET'S GO.
GENTLE-MEN.
ボッ
BOPH

TO BE CONTINUED

ORDER 27 / END

KOHTA HIRANO IS SO HAPPY ABOUT VOLUME 4 GOING ON SALE THAT HE'S CHANGED INTO KOROSUKE AND GONE OFF TO ATTACK COMMODORE PERRY'S OFFSHORE SHIPS WHILE SINGING "FIRST KISS." (TWO SECONDS LATER, A CANNON BLASTS HIM TO BITS.)

*NOTE: KOROSUKE IS A ROBOT CHARACTER FROM FUJIKO F. FUJIO'S STORY "KITERETSU'S ENCYCLOPEDIA."

HOBBIES: BEING OBNOXIOUS, BEATING OFF

FAVORITE PIRATES: THE BLACK CAT PIRATES

*NOTE: THIS IS A REFERENCE TO THE ANIME "ONE PIECE."

FAVORITE ACTOR: EDWARD NORTON
–THE ULTRA-LAME GUY IN "PULP FICTION"

*EDITOR'S NOTE: EDWARD NORTON WASN'T ACTUALLY IN "PULP FICTION."...ahem. MAYBE HE'S REFERRING TO FRANK WHALEY?

IN "SISTER PRINCESS," YOUR FAVORITE WAY FOR THEM TO SAY "OLDER BROTHER":

WHEN THE HEROIC CHOHI YOKUTOKU-LIKE SISTER SAYS IN AN UNBELIEVABLY THICK VOICE...

"ELDER SIBLING!!"

■ "DADDY'S GOT YOUR TWO FAVORITE GOLD BALLS RIGHT HERRRRE!" (WHICH MEANS "HELLO" IN ADACHI WARD DIALECT). GOOD EVENING. THIS IS *KOHTA HIRANO*. (SOUNDING LIKE *BOSS YAMAMORI*). AND SO HERE WE HAVE VOLUME 4. HERE IT IS, SEE? AS ALWAYS I WROTE IT AND DREW IT ANY WAY I FELT LIKE. YEAH I DID, SEE? AND AS ALWAYS IT TOOK A YEAR TO RELEASE ONE BOOK SO I GUESS I'M BOTH TRYING HARD AND GOOFING OFF FROM NOW ON, TOO. JUST KIDDING. JUST KIDDING, SEE?

■ A LOT'S HAPPENED THIS PAST YEAR. THE UCHIMOTO GANG PLEDGED LOYALTY WITH THE AKASHI GANG OVER SAKÉ. EDA CAME BACK FROM PRISON AND WENT ON A RAMPAGE. TAKUBON STOLE SOME SCRAP TO SELL, THEN BOUGHT A COLOR TV FROM SOME LADY. KAT-CHAN FROM OTOMO, WITH A WOODEN SWORD IN ONE HAND, THREW DYNAMITE INTO A BIKE RACE AND WAS SHOT WITH A MAGNUM BY KINYA KITAOHJI. THE SAME KINYA KITAOHJI WAS SUPPOSED TO HAVE KILLED HIMSELF WITH A PISTOL IN A DESERTED HOUSE, BUT INSTEAD HE SHOWED UP LIKE IT WAS NOTHING AND UNIFIED THE HIROSHIMA YAKUZA. HIROKI MATSUKATA FELL INTO BAD HEALTH, TURNED INTO DEMONFACE, AND WAS SHOT TO DEATH. SHINGO YAMASHIRO WAS SHOT TO DEATH, HIROKI MATSUKATA WAS SHOT TO DEATH AGAIN, ASAO KOIKE WAS SHOT TO DEATH, TAKUBON WAS SHOT TO DEATH, AND KUNIE TANAKA WAS SHOT TO DEATH. A LOT'S HAPPENED, SEE? ABOUT HIROSHIMA YAKUZA QUARRELS, YOU CAN'T JUST FIX IT ALL WITH CASH. IF THAT WAS THE CASE, WHY DON'T THEY ALL JUST LIVE OFF PUSSY JUICE? OTOMO-*KUN*, OOOOTOMO-*KUN*, THE MURAOKA GANG'S GOTTA SAVE FACE TOO, YEAH?! AND SPEAKIN' A' THEM MURAOKA GUYS, I'M GETTIN' PRET-TY SICK OF 'EM! Y'SHOULD TRY STANDIN' DOWNWIND OF 'EM SOMETIME! THEY CAN ALL GO JERK OFF AN' HAVE ENOUGH HONOR TO HANG THEMSELVES! YEAHHHH! OHH! OHHHH! I'M TELLIN' YOU, IF MURAOKA'S GETTIN' FAT OFF THE DOUGH FROM THE BIKE RACE TRACK, WE'RE TOO LATE! AND YOU KNOW WHAT MURAOKA DID?! HE SPREAD MY BOSS KAGEURA'S NAME AROUND SO NOW HE CAN'T EVEN WALK AROUND HIROSHIMA. WHAT THE HELL'S WIT' THAT?! HUHHH?! UWAHAHAHAHAHA. WHY DON'T HE JUST STAY HOLED UP HERE, HUH?! OWWW OW OW OW OW. WHAT, AGAIN?! SEE HOW YOU LIKE IT!

GET 'EM!! KILL 'EM!! THE BIG KILLERS OF THE BLOODY HIROSHIMA DISPUTE.

HIROSHIMA LIFE-AND-DEATH STRUGGLE TALE.

CHARACTER DESCRIPTIONS

~~HIRONO GANG BOSS; SHOZO HIRONO~~

■ FIRST LIEUTENANT TUBALCAIN ALHAMBRA

DOING TIME FOR KILLING THE DOI GANG BOSS IN KURE. BECOMES PRISON BUDDY OF YAMANAKA, WHO'S IN THE JOINT FOR ASSAULT. RECEIVES A PARDON AND GOES ON PAROLE, AND RETURNS TO KURE AND STARTS THE HIRONO GANG.

WEAPONS: PLAYING CARDS. HE GOT BURNT UP.

VOICE ACTOR: BUNTA SUGAWARA.

~~OTOMO GANG GANG BOSS; KATSUTOSHI OTOMO~~

■ FIRST LIEUTENANT RIP VAN WINKLE

RACKETEER. A MEMBER OF THE OTOMO ALLIANCE, BUT IS KICKED OUT FOLLOWING INSURGENT ACTIVITY THEN AUDACIOUSLY GETS BACK IN ALONG WITH FRIENDS FROM A YOUTH GANG. SHOT BY HIT MAN YAMANAKA AND ARRESTED.

VOICE ACTOR: SHINICHI CHIBA.

WEAPONS: WOODEN SWORD & TNT.

~~MURAOKA GANG GANG BOSS; MASAHARU YAMANAKA~~

WARRANT OFFICER SCHRÖDINGER

AFTER SERVING TWO YEARS IN PRISON FOR COMMITTING ASSAULT, GOES AFTER OTOMO ALLIANCE RACKETEER KATSUTOSHI AND HIS YOUTH GANG IN HIROSHIMA. BY WAY OF THIS RETALIATION BECOMES THE MURAOKA GANG'S HIT MAN.

WEAPON: MAGNUM.

VOICE ACTOR: KINYA KITAOHJI.

MAGNUM

YAMAMORI GANG GANG BOSS; YOSHIO YAMAMOTO

WHILE DISPLAYING HIS INFLUENCE OVER THE MANY ENTERPRISES IN KURE HE CONTROLS, HE FORCES HIS OLD HENCHMAN HIRONO TO DO DIRTY JOBS. WORKING BEHIND THE SCENES IN THE HIROSHIMA DISPUTE, HE HAS DEALINGS WITH BOTH THE MURAOKA AND OTOMO GANGS...

PAPERWORK HUMANITY
LUKE'S
AND JAN'S
HATE THE HATER CORNER
BAM BAM BAM
JAAAAAN! IT'S ME! IT'S YOUR BIG BROTHER!
I JUST GOT BACK! OPEN THE DOOR!
ドン ドン
CLATA
ガラ
REALLYYY? ARE YOU REALLY MY REAL BROTHER?
IF YOU'RE MY REAL BROTHER, YOU SHOULD BE UP TO THIS...
VOICE ACTOR: KOJI NAKAMOTO
DO YOUR "MARIE ANTOINETTE."
MUMBLE
IF THEY HAVE NO BREAD...
...THEN LET THEM EAT SHIT.
OH YEAAAAH TALK ABOUT STUCK UP!
YOU ARE MY BIG BROTHER!
HAH HAH HAH HAHHH!
VOICE ACTOR: IKARIYA

AND SO, THIS IS VOLUME FOUR.
THIS IS A RISKY DEAL. IT MEANS THIS MANGA IS PLUNGING INTO ITS FOURTH YEAR.
THE ART STYLE IS TOTALLY DIFFERENT FROM WHEN IT STARTED, TOO.
ESPECIALLY THAT WRECK ALUCARD.
SEEMS IT EVEN GOT MADE INTO AN ANIME.
THAT'S ANIME, MAN. ANIME.
DOKABEN, MAN. DOKABEN.
NO, DOKABEN IS SOMETHING ELSE.
WELL IN ANY CASE, IT'S SOMETHING TO BE HAPPY ABOUT.
BY THE WAY, IF YOU WRITE "ANIME-KA" (TURNED INTO ANIME)...
...LIKE "ANI-MEKA" (MECHA BIG BROTHER)...
IT'D BE LIKE THIS.
NOW THAT'S PRETTY SWEET.
CHUNK
DEATH.
~THE END~

HELLSING

KOHTA HIRANO

The manga that spawned the internationally popular anime! Thrill to the exploits of the secretive Hellsing Organization in their attempts to defend queen and country against a host of supernatural foes.

These new edition volumes present updated translations to even more accurately depict the beauty and mayhem of Kohta Hirano's outrageous universe!

VOLUME 1
ISBN 978-1-50673-850-5
$14.99

VOLUME 2
ISBN 978-1-50673-851-2
$14.99

VOLUME 3
ISBN 978-1-50673-852-9
$14.99

VOLUME 4
ISBN 978-1-50673-853-6
$14.99

DARK HORSE MANGA

AVAILABLE AT YOUR LOCAL COMICS SHOP OR BOOKSTORE
TO FIND A COMICS SHOP IN YOUR AREA, VISIT COMICSHOPLOCATOR.COM
For more information or to order direct, visit darkhorse.com